How to
Break Software

A Practical Guide to Testing

How to
Break Software

A Practical Guide to Testing

James A. Whittaker

Addison
Wesley

Boston San Francisco New York
London Toronto Sydney Tokyo Singapore Madrid
Mexico City Munich Paris Cape Town Hong Kong Montreal

Senior Acquisitions Editor	Maite Suarez-Rivas
Executive Editor	Susan Hartman Sullivan
Executive Marketing Manager	Michael Hirsch
Assistant Editor	Lisa Hogue
Production Supervisor	Marilyn Lloyd
Project Manangement	Keith Henry/Dartmouth Publishing
Composition and Art	Dartmouth Publishing
Copyeditor	Dan Cubias
Proofreader	Brooke Albright
Text Design	Sandra Rigney/Joyce Cosentino Wells
Cover Design	Night & Day Design
Cover Illustration	Stephen Foster courtesy of Artville © 2003
Design Manager	Gina Hagen Kolenda
Prepress and Manufacturing	Caroline Fell

Access the latest information about Addison-Wesley titles from our World Wide Web site:
http://www.aw.com/cs

Library of Congress Cataloging-in-Publication Data

Whittaker, James A., 1965–
    How to break software : a practical guide to testing : an example-rich explanation of how to effectively test software that anyone can understand and use immediately / James A. Whittaker.
      p. cm.
    Includes bibliographical references and index.
    ISBN 0-201-79619-8
    1. Computer software—Testing. I. Title.

QA76.76.T48 W47 2002
005.1'4—dc21   2002018693

ISBN 0-201-79619-8
    8910-HAM-06

Dedication

The testers and developers whose skill is embedded in this book are far too numerous to mention. However, there are some who have invested so many hours discussing, debating, and arguing this material that I would be remiss if I didn't thank them personally. My deepest thanks go to James Tierney, Dave Ladd, George Stathakopoulis, Harry Robinson, Bj Rollison, Noel Nyman, and Chris Walker of Microsoft; Mike Houghtaling and Steve Atkin of IBM; Sam Guckenheimer of Rational; Andres De Vivanco; Ibrahim El-Far, Dr. Alan Jorgensen, Scott Chase, Florence Mottay, Nikhil Nilakantan, Dr. Shirley Becker, and Dr. Cem Kaner of Florida Tech.

Mostly, I dedicate this book to my students at Florida Tech. It was here that these techniques were field-tested by young (and not so young), eager minds. I thank my students for their input, their bugs, their enthusiasm, their challenges, their insight, and most of all their help in making Florida Tech a great place to test software.

Preface

About This Book

This book contains little or no testing theory. There are enough books out there on testing theory and too few books about how good testers *actually do* testing. So I wrote such a book. I have attempted to get inside the heads of the best testers I have ever met and document the best techniques to figure out where the bugs are and the most effective ways to find them so that a quality product gets released. My secondary goal is for this book to be fun to read and the techniques involved fun to apply. I love to break software. I hope my enthusiasm for this craft made it to the pages of this text.

About This Book's Audience

It may sound like a sales pitch, but there is something in this book for everyone. It is written in a tutorial fashion that will appeal to beginners, yet the most seasoned testing veteran can appreciate its unique content. Of course, my current career as a university professor means that I also had students in mind as I wrote this. I use this book in undergraduate and graduate testing courses. It is important to learn how to be a good tester and go beyond the basic theory.

About This Book's Examples

This book shows screen snaps of real error messages and odd behavior (dare I say "bugs"?) from actual software applications. These examples are included to illustrate the attack techniques taught in this book. Some of them are great bugs, and some are just minor annoyances. The main purposes of the examples are to teach and to illustrate. They are not meant as examples of great bugs (though some certainly are), nor are they meant to poke fun at the companies who produce the applications. Indeed, I was careful to choose applications that are market leaders and, therefore, immediately recognizable by most readers. Furthermore, each example is from an application produced by a company I regularly deal with and whose development practices and culture I respect and admire.

I encourage readers to use caution when applying the techniques in this book or reproducing the bugs from the screen snaps. Many of the attacks will crash the applications they target. Be sure to save your work before you try the attacks to ensure you don't lose any important data.

About This Book's Organization

How to Break Software is organized into four parts.

Part 1 is an introduction to the field of software breaking and is geared toward teaching an understanding of software and the complex environment in which it operates. It is crucial for software testers to understand their software's environment so that they are aware of what their software is doing internally and how it interacts with its environment. Without such understanding, it is difficult to be a successful software breaker.

Part 2 details very specific attacks that can be applied through a user interface. Whether that interface is a GUI or a programmatic API, this section will show you how to attack the software from that interface, when to apply each attack, and why and how the attack is successful at breaking software. This part will probably be the one you refer to most often as you conduct attack campaigns against your software targets.

Part 3 discusses testing issues for nonhuman system interfaces (that is, how to test the file system, OS, and software interfaces of your application). Attack strategies are discussed. A new tool called HEAT, the Hostile Environment Application Tester, is introduced. You'll find "Canned HEAT" on the CD-ROM that comes with this book. Canned HEAT allows testers to proactively test system interfaces with a technique called runtime fault injection.

Part 4 is a conclusion that makes the point that software testing is never really mastered. Instead, it requires the constant learning and acquisition of new skills. Two fun and lesson-filled exercises that we conduct at Florida Tech are described in this chapter. You can apply them at your lab. They are guaranteed to put fun and learning into any software testing regime!

Three appendixes provide specific resources for software breakers. Appendix A discusses runtime fault injection. Appendix B describes the features of Canned HEAT, an easy-to-use fault injection tool that is on the companion CD-ROM. Appendix C is a reprint of a paper originally published in *IEEE SOFTWARE* that describes the general software testing process. These appendixes supplement the book's contents and can be read on their own or as additional reference material for this book. The glossary contains definitions of commonly used programming terms.

About This Book's Contents

How to Break Software is a departure from conventional testing, in which testers prepare a written test plan and use it as a script when testing the software. Tests are planned in advanced and executed in rote fashion. The testing techniques in this book are as flexible as conventional testing is rigid. Flexibility is needed in software projects in which requirements change, bugs become features, and schedule pressures force plans to be reassessed.

Software testing is not such an exact science that one can determine what to test in advance, execute the plan, and be done with it. This would take god-like powers of foresight. Instead of a plan, intelligence, insight, experience, and a nose for where the bugs are hiding should guide testers. This book can help testers develop this insight.

As a long-time advocate of test planning and automated test execution, my first forays into such freestyle testing were as a skeptic. However, the facts were simply against me. Smart people doing exploratory testing have found all the best bugs I have ever seen. These same smart people would outperform the best test automation, not by a small margin but by an order of magnitude. Whenever a project was in trouble and serious testing was needed, it was always the smartest testers who were called in, not the test plans or the test automation. Whenever crucial ship decisions needed to be made, smart managers would ignore the disposition of the test plan in favor of the most experienced testers' opinions.

I was soon convinced that my grandiose research agenda of totally automated testing needed to be seriously reconsidered. I became intensely interested in those testers who knew the product and found all the bugs. I witnessed these folks routinely go off-script and manage to lose the official test plan under a pile of documents on their desk. When questioned, they invariably responded, "That plan ain't where the bugs are."

The techniques presented in this book not only allow testers to go off-script, they encourage them to do so. Don't blindly follow a document that may be out of date or was written before the product was even testable. Instead, use your head! Open your eyes! Think a little, test a little, and think a little more.

However, do not get the idea that I am against planning or documentation. This book simply teaches on-the-fly planning while you are testing. Do not get the idea that automation is discouraged. There are many repetitive, complex tasks that require good tools (indeed, one such tool is shipped with this book on the companion CD). However, tools are never used as a replacement for intelligence. Testers do the thinking and use tools to collect data that helps them explore applications more efficiently and effectively.

If this book has a motto, it might be

Know your product, think on your feet, and let your experience guide you.

It might be even simpler:

Brain on, eyes open . . . test!

I have long studied such testing in earnest. I did this by watching people and studying their bugs. What do the best testers do to find bugs? What do the best bugs have in common? Are there ways to generalize the actions of experienced testers that will help inexperienced testers be better?

It is my intention to capture the best ideas and testing strategies of the best testers I have met, and document these ideas in such a way that novice testers can study them and become better testers. If this material does not accomplish that goal, it is the fault of my meager communication skills alone, not a reflection of my research subjects' skill. Anything that is good in this book comes from the work of those colleagues who were closely studied. I thank them for sharing their bugs and their insights. Anything that is wrong with this book is entirely my own doing. Documenting testing brilliance is hard for a mere mortal like me.

About This Book's Supplements

This book comes with a CD that contains two very useful testing tools that were written by faculty and students at Florida Tech. Canned HEAT and Holodeck Lite are runtime monitoring and fault injection tools that run on the Windows NT family of platforms. Both tools are easy to use and are explained in detail in Part 3 of this book and in the appendixes.

In addition, *www.HowToBreakSoftware.com* is your online gateway to the latest tool updates, bug stories, and technology announcements related to the discipline of breaking software.

James A. Whittaker
Melbourne, Florida
August 2001

 **Acknowledgments**

I would like to express my appreciation to the following reviewers:

Jim Bieman — *Colorado State University*
Neil Bitzenhofer — *University of Minnesota*
John Callahan — *Sphere Software Corporation*
Barbara Endicott-Popovsky — *Endicott Consulting, Inc.*
Bill Junk — *University of Idaho*
Gail Kaiser — *Columbia University*
Danny Kopec — *Brooklyn College*
Bruce Maxim — *University of Michigan-Dearborn*
James McDonald — *Monmouth University*
Rob Sabourin — *AmiBug.Com, Inc.*
Ye Wu — *George Mason University*

Chapter Summaries

PART 1: INTRODUCTION

Chapter 1–A Fault Model to Guide Software Testing

This chapter teaches you how to think about software behavior. It presents a novel perspective on software behavior: By understanding what software is doing, we can understand how it can do it wrong. This understanding is called a fault model, and it can lead us to specific attacks that find bugs and help us exercise the important behaviors that must work for the product to be successfully released.

PART 2: USER INTERFACE ATTACKS

Chapter 2–Testing from the User Interface: Inputs and Outputs

This chapter will probably be the one that you read the most and gives you the most benefit. It gives very specific advice on what to do when you are sitting at your keyboard trying to figure out which inputs to apply. It also tells you how to make your software generate interesting output. This chapter is black box testing at its best.

Chapter 3–Testing from the User Interface: Data and Computation

This chapter covers what is often called "gray box testing" because it deals with issues somewhere between white box and black box. Although source code is not needed, the attacks presented teach testers to look beyond the software's interface to understand internal data and computation. The focus is on attacks that are specific to breaking data and computation constraints.

PART 3: SYSTEM INTERFACE ATTACKS

Chapter 4–Testing from the File System Interface

Software can fail when it interacts with data files. This chapter focuses on the problems and solutions of testing the file system interface. Canned HEAT, the tool provided on the companion CD, is first used in this chapter.

Chapter 5–Testing from the Software/OS Interface

Software almost always uses other software to perform some work for it. When external software resources fail or behave unexpectedly, our own software can break too. This chapter discusses the testing problems associated with application interoperability and uses Canned HEAT to provide insight into the testing of software-to-software interfaces.

PART 4: CONCLUSION

Chapter 6—Some Parting Advice

Sometimes it isn't technique or technology that makes a great testing team. This chapter discusses some of the best test-team building exercises that I have come across. They are challenging and productive ways to make your job more fun and your team more productive.

APPENDIXES

Annotated Glossary of Programming Terms

Ever listen to developers and wonder what the heck they are talking about? This chapter removes the mystery by providing straightforward explanations of things such as APIs, delimiters, exception handlers, controls, and oracles. You can read this chapter first or refer to it whenever an unfamiliar term pops up in the book.

Appendix A—Runtime Fault Injection

This paper is included to help the reader gain additional insight into using HEAT to simulate faulty operational environments for software. Although much of the advice in this chapter is sprinkled throughout Chapters 3 and 4, it is included here for a single comprehensive reference point.

Appendix B—Using HEAT: The Hostile Environment Application Tester

HEAT stands for Hostile Environment Application Tester. It provides a mechanism to easily trip exceptions (there's one of those terms described in the glossary) and force error code to execute. HEAT can be used to simulate a faulty network, low memory, a full hard drive, or any number of other common failure scenarios. This appendix contains a nicely formatted and printed version of the "Help" files contained under Canned HEAT's "Help" menu.

Appendix C—What is Software Testing? And Why is it So Hard?

This is a standalone paper that was published in IEEE Software (Volume 17, Number 1, January/February 2000). It is included because it introduces other phases of testing that are not covered in this book (for example, domain analysis, model-based testing, regression testing, and software reliability estimation). This paper is meant to be a complete survey of the problems one will encounter when testing software and a summary of the solutions available to the tester. With hope, it will whet your appetite for more knowledge about software testing that is beyond the scope of this book.

Table of Contents

Dedication   *v*
Preface   *vii*
Acknowledgments   *xi*
Chapter Summaries   *xiii*

PART 1   INTRODUCTION   **1**
Chapter 1   **A Fault Model to Guide Software Testing**   3
The Purpose of Software Testing   3
Understanding Software Behavior   4
Understanding Software's Environment   6
    The Human User   8
    File System User   9
    The Operating System User   10
    The Software User   11
Understanding Software's Capabilities   11
    Testing Input   12
    Testing Output   13
    Testing Data   13
    Testing Computation   14
Summary and Conclusion   14
Exercises   15
References   16

PART 2   USER INTERFACE ATTACKS   **17**
Chapter 2   **Testing from the User Interface:**
              Inputs and Outputs   **19**
Using the Fault Model to Guide Testing   19
Exploring the Input Domain   19
    Attack 1: Apply inputs that force all the
        error messages to occur   20
    Attack 2: Apply inputs that force the
        software to establish default values   25
    Attack 3: Explore allowable character sets
        and data types   28
    Attack 4: Overflow input buffers   34

Attack 5: Find inputs that may interact
and test combinations of their values   37

Attack 6: Repeat the same input or series
of inputs numerous times   39

Exploring Outputs   42

Attack 7: Force different outputs to be
generated for each input   42

Attack 8: Force invalid outputs to be generated   44

Attack 9: Force properties of an output to change   47

Attack 10: Force the screen to refresh   51

Conclusion   54
Exercises   55
References   55

Chapter 3   **Testing from the User Interface:
Data and Computation**   **57**

Testing Inside the Box   57
Exploring Stored Data   57

Attack 11: Apply inputs using a
variety of initial conditions   58

Attack 12: Force a data structure
to store too many or too few values   60

Attack 13: Investigate alternate ways
to modify internal data constraints   63

Exploring Computation and Feature Interaction   67

Attack 14: Experiment with invalid
operand and operator combinations   67

Attack 15: Force a function to call
itself recursively   71

Attack 16: Force computation results
to be too large or too small   73

Attack 17: Find features that share
data or interact poorly   75

Conclusion   78
Exercises   78

PART 3   **SYSTEM INTERFACE ATTACKS**   **81**

Chapter 4   **Testing from the File System Interface**   **83**

Attacking Software from the File System Interface   83
Media-based Attacks   83

Attack 1: Fill the file system to its capacity | 84
Attack 2: Force the media to be busy
　　or unavailable | 89
Attack 3: Damage the media | 94
File-based Attacks | 95
Attack 4: Assign an invalid file name | 96
Attack 5: Vary file access permissions | 99
Attack 6: Vary or corrupt file contents | 100
Summary and Conclusion | 103
Exercises | 104

Chapter 5　Testing from the Software/OS Interface | **105**
Attacking Software from Software Interfaces | 105
Record-and-Simulate Attacks | 106
Inject faults that cause all error-handling code
　　to be executed and exceptions to be tripped | 106
Inject faults that can be readily staged in the testing lab | 106
Inject faults that might realistically occur in the field | 107
Observe-and-Fail Attacks | 116
Conclusion | 120
Exercises | 120

PART 4　　CONCLUSION | **121**
Chapter 6　Some Parting Advice | **123**
You'll Never Know Everything | 123
Bug Hunts | 124
Friday Afternoon Bug Fests | 125
Conclusion | 126
References | 126

APPENDIXES | **127**
Annotated Glossary of Programming Terms | **129**

**Appendix A　Testing Exception and Error Cases
　　　　　　Using Runtime Fault Injection** | **135**
Introduction | 135
A Mechanism for Runtime Fault Injection | 136
Fault Selection | 138
Pattern-based Fault Injection | 139
Systematic Call-based Fault Injection | 148

Conclusions   150
Acknowledgments   151
References   151

Appendix B Using HEAT: The Hostile
              Environment Application Tester   **153**
Canned HEAT User Guide   153
The Application Band   153
The Monitor Band   154
Fault-Injection Bands and Their Functionality   154
The Network Band   155
Disk Storage   156
Memory   157

Appendix C What is Software Testing?
              And Why is it So Hard?   **159**
Introduction   159
The Software Testing Process   160
Phase One: Modeling the Software's Environment   160
Phase Two: Selecting Test Scenarios   163
Phase Three: Running and Evaluation Test Scenarios   165
Phase Four: Measuring Testing Progress   167
Conclusion   169
References   169

The Software Testing Problem   **170**

Index   **175**

PART 1

Introduction

CHAPTER 1
A Fault Model to Guide Software Testing

The Purpose of Software Testing

Many people test software for many different reasons. Most of these reasons have a descriptive name. We might test to decide whether our organization should acquire a product. This is called *acceptance testing.* We might test to determine whether a product meets an implementation standard. This is called *conformance testing.* We might test to determine how easy a product is to use. This is called *usability testing.* The list goes on and includes *performance testing, reliability testing, robustness testing,* and other terms.

The many forms of software testing share some common elements:

1. Each requires that testers work from a description of the product's behavior. This can be a written specification, a requirements document, a product documentation or user manual, the source code, or the working executable. Obviously, it is desirable to have as much accurate information about the product as possible. However, in some cases the only things available are the working executable and a general idea of how the product should work.

2. Each requires that the product be executed in a real or simulated environment. The fact that we work with a functioning executable distinguishes testing from code reviews and inspections, which can be employed statically on a product before it is compiled and linked.

3. Each implies that the product's functionality is explored in a methodical way, that the outcome of the test is positive (the test was a success) or negative (the test failed), and that we can judge the difference. Indeed, distinguishing a failed test from a successful test is the whole point: We must know what we are looking for and be able to tell when we've found it.

All forms of testing contain these elements and differ mainly in *intent* and in how some of the details are handled. Independent of these details and intentions, however, is that software testing requires execution and exploration of a product's functionality in a methodical, intelligent manner. This book concentrates on this core testing technology: exploration of software functionality in an intelligent manner, no matter how much or how little documentation we have.

Thus the difference between users and testers is that testers have clear goals. Simply banging on the keyboard is the task of rookie testers who are no better than untrained users stumbling across the occasional bug. Setting goals that allow us to zero in on bugs and expose poor design efficiently and effectively is the domain of trained, skilled testers.

Readers familiar with the testing literature will notice a marked absence of written test plans in this book. Instead, I opt for a more "freestyle" testing. Testers are not tethered to a written test plan that they must execute in rote fashion. However, we will not be ad hoc either. Software testing is about intelligence. Experience, procedures, and knowledge of how the application works and its possible faults guide testers. Anyone can stumble across bugs in software. This is called *luck* (if you're a tester you might call it luck, if you're a user you may have a different name for it). But luck is a poor substitute for skill and will rarely be enough to ensure a well-tested product.

Good testers do not rely on luck. Rather, they set clear, concrete, achievable goals for their tests and the next goal until no stone is left unturned (or a business concern forces management to a premature release decision). Setting such goals and systematically exploring until they are achieved is the hallmark of good testing.

This book discusses software testing in this context: what testing goals should be and how to explore a software's functionality to meet these goals. Doing so will allow us to find bugs, ensure that our application meets its requirements, and satisfy the intent of our testing.

Understanding Software Behavior

Building nontrivial software is an enormously difficult endeavor and usually results in software that fails once it gets fielded. Developers must work on ways to make programming less error-prone, and testers must focus on ways to test that software does what it is supposed to do without failure. Unfortunately for testers, there are too many inputs, input variables, input combinations, and internal software states (configurations of stored data) to test everything. Some functionality must remain untested. Much of the challenge of testing is choosing what to test and what to leave untested.

To perform this crucial decision-making process effectively, testers need to understand what software is doing as it executes and what things could cause the software to fail. The best testers I know are the ones who have developed an intuition for what causes software to fail. They use this intuition to guide them as they think through test scenarios. In other words, they know where bugs commonly hide and have figured out how to expose them efficiently.

The technical term for this intuition that guides testers is a *fault model* because it provides a model or framework to discuss how and why faults in the code can manifest themselves as failures when the software executes. It is important that testers form an accurate fault model and use it during testing to ensure that the most likely hiding spots for bugs are thoroughly examined. In other words, a fault model allows us to select tests that are most likely to expose embedded software faults.

We will discuss a general software fault model that applies to all software whether it is a complete hack, object-oriented, web-enabled, or developed in a single programming language or many languages.[1] The fault model takes into account the differences in implementation that make each software product unique.

I think the fault model testers need to learn and internalize is based on two fundamental issues concerning the software we test.

First, we must be very familiar with the *environment* in which our software operates. We must understand the other systems (for example, humans, hardware, or software) that communicate with our application and the specific ways in which this communication can occur. A common cause of software field failure is miscommunication between the software and its environment.

Software environments are much more complex than "software works on a computer." Indeed, many developers fail to understand the environment in which their code operates. They trust users when they shouldn't, they fail to validate data when they should, they read from files without checking their contents for validity, and so forth. As testers, it is our job to catch these mistakes; to do so, we must understand software environments even better than developers do.

In the following section, we will describe a generalized software environment and discuss some of the testing issues involved in the types of interfaces through which software communicates with its environment. This will allow us to explore the interaction between software and its environment to discover which interactions cause the software to fail.

Second, testers must understand the *capabilities* that their application possesses. All software exists to provide functionality and service to its users. Testers must understand this functionality and how users supply input to make the software perform its prescribed tasks. The variation of these inputs and the verification of the resultant behavior of the software is what testing is all about.

Software's capabilities are more complicated than they might seem. Indeed, what is software capable of doing? What are the constituent building blocks upon which software is constructed? Software is much

---

[1] Some fault models are specific to certain programming languages (for example, Reference 1 is a fault model for Fortran, Reference 2 discusses specific fault models for C, and Reference 3 covers Ada), and other fault models address problems specific to programming paradigms. Binder's book (Reference 4) addresses a fault model for object-oriented programming.

more than predicates and assignment statements. If we understand the facts about software's capabilities, we will be in a much better position to test it thoroughly.

In the following sections, I discuss software environments and the general capabilities that all software possesses. This will set the stage for later chapters that will demonstrate how testing can focus on these capabilities to expose faults and force software to exhibit its functionality efficiently and effectively.

Understanding Software's Environment

Software exists in an environment in which it communicates with its users by accepting inputs and producing outputs. Although it isn't intuitive for novice testers, humans are *not* users of most software systems. In fact, humans cannot submit inputs directly to software applications. Instead, humans use hardware devices like a keyboard or mouse whose inputs are processed by device drivers (a special class of software that *can* communicate with hardware). These inputs pass through layers of operating system application programming interfaces (API) until one such API generates an event that the application under test receives. In reality, application software receives input only from the operating system (OS).

On modern computers, application software resides completely within the care of the host operating system. No input touches the application without going through the OS, which delivers each output to its ultimate destination. So the popular notion that input from human users is the main aspect of testing is naïve and inaccurate. Instead, the environment in which application software executes is similar to the diagram in Fig. 1.1. This figure shows that there are four classes of users: the operating system kernel provides memory, file pointers, and services such as time and date functions; the file system provides data stored in binary or text format; the human interface is implemented as a set of APIs that gets inputs from the keyboard, mouse, or other devices; and other software systems (for example, databases, runtime libraries, etc.) supply inputs and data as return values of API calls.

FIGURE 1.1 | An application works within an operating system. The operating system acts as intermediary with each of the users.

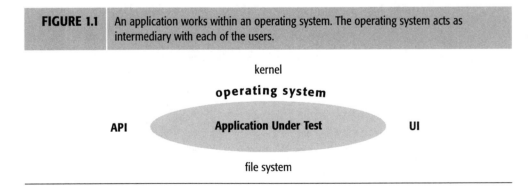

kernel

operating system

API **Application Under Test** UI

file system

Consider the interaction that occurs between an application and its environment when the application is invoked. The scenario goes something like what is shown in Table 1.1:

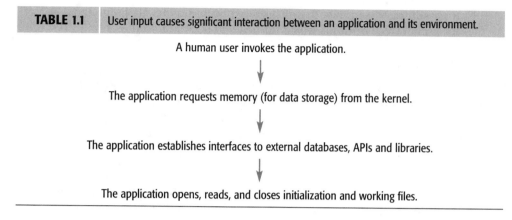

TABLE 1.1	User input causes significant interaction between an application and its environment.

A human user invokes the application.

↓

The application requests memory (for data storage) from the kernel.

↓

The application establishes interfaces to external databases, APIs and libraries.

↓

The application opens, reads, and closes initialization and working files.

Thus just the simple act of invoking an application causes activity between the application and its four classes of interfaces. While the application is being used, such interaction is pervasive.

For example, the ubiquitous Microsoft PowerPoint®, a complex and large application for making presentations and slide shows, makes fifty-nine calls to twenty-nine different functions (excluding GetTickCount, which is called nearly seven hundred times) of the Windows® kernel upon invocation. That means a single input from a human user invoking PowerPoint causes a flurry of undercover communication to be transferred to and from the operating system kernel.

Certainly, invocation is a special input and requires a great deal of setup and data initialization. However, other operations are demanding on low-level resources. When PowerPoint opens a file, twelve kernel functions are called seventy-three times (once again excluding GetTickCount, which is called more than five hundred times). When PowerPoint changes a font, two kernel functions are called ten times.

These are only the calls to the operating system kernel. PowerPoint also uses a number of external resources (dynamically linked libraries), including mso9.dll, gdi32.dll, user32.dll, advapi32.dll, comctl32.dll, and ole32.dll, in the same manner as the kernel. It is easy to see that the amount of communication between an application and its system users dwarfs visible human input.

PowerPoint isn't alone. All applications use external resources. Understanding what these resources are and being able to reproduce and simulate interaction with them is a fundamental task for software testers.

Simulating a software's environment is very tough to do. Just getting each user to supply the input you want, when you want it, is formidable. How does one get the operating system to return a specific error code? How does one effectively modify binary files and get them to look the way you intend? How does one make GUI controls fail? How does one coax other software to return the data you specified? The challenge that each of these interfaces presents to testers is discussed next.

The Human User

Although most software that you will test does not actually get stimulated by a human user (the exception being device drivers, which receive human input through a hardware device), treating the human as a user is a useful abstraction. Two human interfaces are common for software: the GUI and the API.

Inputs delivered via GUI controls

GUIs (and their older cousins, the menu-driven interface and the command line interface) present special but well-studied testing problems. GUIs work as a collection of controls that a human user stimulates via the mouse or keyboard. This causes events and data to be passed back to the software under test. Some controls, like buttons, have very simple events that they can pass. Other controls have not only numerous events but also data to pass as well (like a list box that returns the string that the user highlights).

Testing data-passing controls is challenging, particularly because in many cases separate controls are used to collect related data. Thus testers must be concerned about discovering these relationships and testing combinations of data that might cause the software to fail.

Another concern is the order in which GUI controls are used. Developers often decide that a user should follow a certain execution path through the software—meaning that they are expected to use certain controls before other controls—and then write code under the assumption that the user will play by these rules. However, unless the interface physically constrains the user to a specified route, users can and will do just about everything. Testers must ensure that the developers used appropriate assumptions about how users will use the software and that the software cannot easily be broken by straying from the expected input sequence.

As testers, it is our job to understand the events and data combinations that originate with human users and ensure that all the interesting cases get tested.

Inputs delivered via programs

Some applications allow developers to be users by exposing internal functionality that other programs can call (that is, an API). In such cases software developers can write programs that execute the application under test. Testing such software means that we must write programs that make the calls to the software under test and vary the allowable parameters and call sequences. Testers must have programming ability to test such software.

Fortunately, the strategy used to test APIs is much the same as that used to test GUIs. Indeed, testing both types of applications provides similar challenges, except that API testers must deal with API calls and parameter selection instead of GUI controls and data. Identifying the data to pass in an API call is no different than deciding what data to type into a GUI control. Choosing parameter combinations and API call sequencing is no different than selecting the order in which GUI controls should be used. The only difference is the delivery mechanism: programs for testing APIs or keyboards for testing GUIs.

For either interface, testers face tough problems. One overwhelming problem is that there are simply too many inputs, input combinations, and input sequences to apply them all. Whether we define an input as a text entry field on a GUI control or as a parameter in an API call, we must be able to select a specific input from a nearly infinite number of choices.

So which inputs are most important? We could select the inputs that real users most commonly apply. However, human users (whether they are programmers or users in the more ordinary sense) are exquisitely difficult to predict, and the risk of guessing the wrong user profile is great. Besides, the number of users is often large enough to guarantee that people whom we do not want to lose as customers will use every single feature. We are stuck with a very tough decision: what to test and what to leave to chance.

In Chapters 2 and 3 we will discuss the issues involved in testing via human interfaces. I will describe in detail a method of selecting tests based on exercising functionality in a methodical, intelligent manner. Our goal is to make software do real work and explore the most likely hiding spots of catastrophic or inconvenient bugs.

The File System User

Almost all software uses binary or text files. For testers, files are users and their contents are inputs. Like the inputs we have already discussed, file contents can be invalid. Files, even binary ones, are easy to change outside the confines of the applications that create and process them. What happens, for example, when a privileged user changes the permissions of a file that another user is editing?

File permissions are just one example of how files can wreak havoc on software applications. The data within a file might be corrupt. Files can contain data that is the wrong type or that is incorrectly formatted. Field delimiters may be misplaced, or fields may be in the wrong order. The file may simply be too large for the application under test to handle.

An application's defenses against corrupt files is usually weak. As long as the file extension is correct, the "magic string" is in place at the top of the file (as an identifier), and the field delimiters are in place, the contents are often read without being checked. Our job as testers is to understand the files and file formats that the software under test processes. Testers must also be able to construct files with the desired content to test for appropriate behavior.

In Chapter 4 we will discuss techniques for testing the file system interface of software and ways in which faults can be injected into files to test the ability of software to handle such situations gracefully.

The Operating System User

As Fig. 1.1 on page 6 shows, the operating system is the only entity that interacts directly with application software. It is the intermediary between all physical users and application software. It also interacts directly with an application by supplying memory, file handles, heap space, and so forth. This part of the operating system is the *kernel*.

The Windows kernel, for example, exports over a thousand different functions, each of which has at least two return values (to indicate success or an error condition). This is a challenge for developers who all too often trust the kernel explicitly. When they allocate memory, they expect memory, not an error code saying, "sorry, it's all gone." Every time memory is allocated, the program has to check the return code for success before continuing its task. If it does not, it will behave unexpectedly or fail when low-memory conditions occur. Our job as testers is to think creatively about the ways that unexpected operating environments will affect the software we are testing and then figure out how to simulate such behavior (that is, to get the operating system to conform to our test plan).

For example, we may want to test that our application works in an acceptable manner in low-memory situations (for example, when it has to compete with other applications for local resources). To achieve this we might stress local resources by running a few dozen applications in the background during a test, hoping that some calls to the kernel will fail. However, by doing so we are creating a debugging nightmare for our developers, who will have a difficult time reproducing and isolating the specific problem in the source code. Furthermore, we may destabilize our system, forcing time-consuming reboots to return to normal tests.

The fundamental problem with system interfaces is that, unlike human user input, system input is *reactive*. In other words, we cannot simply apply system inputs like we apply user inputs by pressing keys and clicking the mouse. System inputs occur outside the direct control of a human tester as the software reacts to user input.

We might, for example, open a file by double-clicking its icon. This action causes the software to request memory and file handles from the kernel. If we want these requests to be denied, we have to do more work. We could rig the environment to fail by artificially stressing the system or manually corrupting files. We could also use system-level debugging tools to force system calls to fail on command. The latter approach is preferable because it helps avoid frequent rebooting and allows developers to easily isolate the exact causal fault.

In Chapters 4 and 5 we will discuss the issues involved in stress testing and demonstrate how debugging tools can be used to aid the process. We will make extensive use of the Hostile Environment Application Tester (HEAT) tools that are available on the companion CD and described in Appendixes A and B.

The Software User

Similar to the operating system user, external software (for example, run-time libraries and third-party components) can be used to store data and perform various and sundry tasks for an application. For example, an application can make SQL queries to an external relational database or use APIs for programming sockets, performing matrix algebra, manipulating strings, or performing any number of commonly reused functions.

As testers we must ensure that our application can handle expected behavior, and reasonable but unexpected behavior, of its external resources. This means we have to consider the data that is passed to our application, the return values and error codes of external resources, and the possible failure scenarios of the resource. Certainly, because we are dealing with *software* we can safely assume that there are bugs in our user! Databases, math libraries, and any other external resource our application may link to or communicate with can fail.

The environment can also affect our software. Disks can get full, or networks can get congested. If we care about how our software performs under such environmental stress, we must be able to recreate these situations in the lab and not allow our users to face them for the first time without knowledge of the possible consequences.

Inputs from software users are discussed in Chapter 5 because they are similar in form and content to operating system issues.

Understanding Software's Capabilities

Despite its well-earned reputation for complexity, software only performs four basic tasks. Although these tasks are straightforward, they can be combined within a single software system to solve very complicated problems. The resulting software can be extremely complex and difficult to test.

Trying to face this complexity in its totality in a massive frontal testing assault is an impossible endeavor and can lead to significant unproductive work. Testers simply get overwhelmed with planning how to test the untestable. Focusing on basic software capabilities often proves to be much more effective. This is the spirit of freestyle testing: fighting many small battles instead of waging all-out war. The idea is to set modest, achievable goals focusing on specific software capabilities. Once testing meets these goals, new goals are established (and so forth) until the software is fully tested (that is, war is waged one battle at a time).

The battle analogy is a useful way to think about software testing. A good wartime general can get into the mind of his enemy, understand what capabilities the enemy possesses, and create ways of disrupting those capabilities. If the enemy's strength is in human troops, attacking supply lines is a useful way of weakening that capability. If its strength is heavy artillery, disrupting communications and remote sensing is a good attack strategy.

Software testers are very much like wartime generals. We too must study the capabilities of our "enemy" (that is, bugs in the *software* and not the developers!) and figure out "attacks" (test cases) that affect the software's ability to perform what it is supposed to do. The major difference is that whether or not we succeed in breaking the software, we have won because a carefully planned and executed attack will either expose a bug or give us confidence that our software works.

In subsequent chapters we will discuss general tactics for attacking the four fundamental capabilities that all software possesses:

1.   Software accepts input from its environment.
2.   Software produces output and transmits it to its environment.
3.   Software stores data internally in one or more data structures.
4.   Software performs computations using input and stored data.

The fault model that will guide us as testers is simple: If software does any of these four things wrong, it fails.

In the next four sections we will discuss these capabilities and the general testing concerns surrounding them. In later chapters we will discuss how specific attacks can be formulated based on the properties of these capabilities.

We begin with input and output, traditionally called *black box testing* because one does not have to be able to see details of the internal implementation to design attacks. Data and computation attacks generally fall under the category of *white box testing* because some knowledge of internals is needed to deploy the attacks. However, we will not require knowledge of source implementation. Instead, we will look through the GUI and surmise enough about the implementation to design some very successful, productive attacks.

Testing Input

Software should only accept input that it can handle. Erroneous and illegal input must be filtered by an interface the software uses (such as a GUI) or by additional error-checking code that is embedded within the software. Software should also know what to do once it gets an input. In particular, it needs to know which input combinations cannot be dealt with even if each individual value may be correct.

Inputs or input combinations that are illegal but get processed anyway (that is, they are not properly filtered at an interface, or they elude error-checking code) will eventually cause the software to fail. This is where testers come in. Our job is to test that our software prevents invalid values from being accepted and that invalid combinations of valid inputs cannot fool the software.

This is an enormous task. If we overlook one value, it may very well be the value that brings the application to its knees. However, the problem is that there are lots of values, and the number of value combinations almost always exceeds our testing resources.

Testing Output

An issue closely resembling the input problem is that of software outputs. Software must generate only those outputs that are acceptable to its users. If our software makes an API call, the call must be well formed and use only parameters within the acceptable range. If our software displays data on an output device for a human user, the data must fit in the defined display area and the screen must be refreshed if necessary. Our software must never pass incorrect values to its users.

Outputs must not only be correct in quantity and format, they must be logically correct. A calendar program that allows the date February 29, 2001, is wrong. Its format and type are fine, but the output is invalid. A tester who doesn't understand the leap-year rule is in a very bad position to find such a bug. Indeed, finding output-related bugs often requires a great deal of domain expertise. Imagine testing a flight-simulator game without understanding how to fly an airplane. Distinguishing between correct and incorrect output would be a huge problem.

Once again testers have an enormously difficult task. We must understand the problem well enough to enumerate wrong answers and try to ensure that such answers cannot be generated.

Testing Data

Software can store input values or the results of computation internally in one or more data structures. This data can be retrieved for use in computation or output generation. Software sets itself up for failure if it stores illegal data. We must be careful to keep our data structures free of such corruption.

In many ways the testing concerns about data are similar to our concerns about input. Data values must be individually acceptable and also live happily with other data that the application under test stores. Thus many of the tests designed for inputs are valid for testing stored data.

However, the nature of stored data is that it is persistent. Not only can it be stored, it can be retrieved and modified. Because software systems are large and complex, any number of internal programs often can modify a particular data structure. If these programs have different rules about what range of values are acceptable for that data or use different assumptions about those values, the software can fail.

Our task as testers is to apply input that targets data structures—add to them, take from them, overflow them, underflow them, and otherwise confuse them into doing something that will cause the system to fail.

Testing Computation

Even if all inputs, outputs, and stored data are kept within their legal limits, these values can still be combined in ways that make the software fail. Even the most elementary computation, $x = x + 1$, can cause a program to crash if it is executed enough times to overflow the memory set aside for the value x. Indeed, computation can only be performed *if* all data used in the computation are correct *and* the value computed falls within an acceptable range.

In addition, a common problem that many programmers struggle with is that of feature interaction. It is not uncommon that certain software features act on shared data. As long as those features are independent, they work fine. However, combine those features, and you might have a recipe for disaster. For example, a module that provides footnote capability for a word processor might work fine by itself on a normal document, but convert the document to a two-column format and these two features might conflict. Footnote capability may very well depend on the fact that the document is *not* dual column. In other words, the computation that occurs to place the footnote in the proper place may not work correctly in dual-column mode. Anticipating all possible feature interactions is a very tall order and illustrates well the point that software testing is a massively complex endeavor.

■■ Summary and Conclusion

Software is tested for many different purposes, but all software testing consists of two main issues: establishing an *environment* in which an application can be tested and testing the *capabilities* of the software in that environment. Testers must understand and replicate the complex environment in which their software exists and exercise its capabilities to ensure proper testing.

The fault model presented in this chapter is based on the environment and capabilities of software. The environment consists of four types of users: the operating system user, the file system user, the human user, and other software users. We must consider all activity that occurs between our software and any of these users to be fair game for testing.

The capabilities of software fall into four general categories: input, output, data, and computation. This fault model requires that each of these four categories be tested to ensure that the software performs as expected.

This book discusses testing in this context. How does one systematically study an application's environment? How does one set up a test environment that is capable of fully exercising the software's capabilities? How does one establish the capabilities of a specific application? How does one test each capability that an application possesses? What makes a good test good and a bad test bad? How much testing is enough?

Each of these questions and a plethora of related testing issues are studied in the following chapters. However, testing is an emerging discipline, and all the answers are not yet forthcoming. We'll study the answers that are out there and discuss what is known about the answers we yet seek.

▪▪ Exercises

Professional testers can use whatever software application they are work-ing on to perform these exercises. Students can choose any application they use frequently. At Florida Tech, we choose an application in advance for our semester-long class, and everyone in the class works on it, usually in teams of two.

Once you have selected your application under test, perform the following exercises.

1. Name the four classes of users for your application.

   a. For each class of user, list several examples of the types of users in the class (for example, a professional writer is a type of human user for a word processor application).

   b. For each class of user, spend at least ten minutes listing all the *inputs* you can think of.

   c. For each class of user, spend at least ten minutes listing all the *outputs* you can think of.

2. What are the four categories of capabilities that your application possesses?

   a. Use your application for at least ten minutes and find as many *data* items as you can. List them.

   b. As you use your application, make a list of its major *features*.

   c. For each feature you noted, make a list of the *computations* that each feature performs.

3. Review the first section of this chapter and reflect on your company's attitude toward the purpose of testing (or if you are a student, reflect on the attitude of your instructor and classmates). Make a list of the purposes you see, rank them from most important to least important (from the point of view of your company), and comment on whether the order is as it should be.

4. The point that GUIs and APIs present the same set of testing problems was made in this chapter. List the testing challenges of a GUI panel that has a number of interrelated text entry fields and "OK/Cancel" buttons. Now describe these challenges if the GUI were rewritten as an API.

▪▪ References

1. K. King and A. J. Offut, "A Fortran Language System for Mutation-based Software Testing," *Software Practice and Experience*, Vol. 21, No. 7, 685-718, July 1991.

2. H. Agrawal, et al. "Design of Mutant Operators for the C Programming Language," *Technical Report* SERC-TR-41-P, Software Engineering Research Center, Purdue University, West Lafayette, IN, March 1989.

3. J. Bowser, "Reference Manual for Ada Mutant Operators," *Technical Report* GIT-SERC-88/02, Department of Computer Science, Georgia Institute of Technology, Atlanta, GA, February 1988.

4. R. Binder, *Testing Object Oriented Systems: Models, Patterns and Tools*, (Addison-Wesley, 1999).

5. J. A. Whittaker, "Software's Invisible Users," *IEEE Software*, Vol. 18, No. 3, 84-88, May/June 2001.

6. J. A. Whittaker and J. M. Voas, "Toward a More Reliable Theory of Software Reliability," *IEEE Computer*, Vol. 33, No. 12, 36-42, December 2000.

PART 2

User Interface Attacks

CHAPTER 2
Testing from the User Interface: Inputs and Outputs

01100010110110110001010100

Using the Fault Model to Guide Testing

Understanding what software does—and how it might fail doing it—is crucial to being an effective tester. The fault model presented in the previous chapter provides insight into developing such an understanding, but a lot of practice is needed to put the fault model to good use.

In this chapter, I present strategies for applying the fault model and discuss in detail the philosophy behind using the model to find bugs in software. I call the strategies for applying the fault model "attacks" because the mindset of attacking the software is an effective learning tool. Particularly in the academic environment in which I work, it is a good way to convince budding developers that testing is a fun way to spend their time.

This chapter covers attacks that are orchestrated from the *user interface* (UI). In later chapters we'll cover attacks from the other three interfaces. I divide UI attacks into four categories, one for each of the capabilities of software: *accepting input, producing output, storing data,* and *performing computation.* The idea is that testers apply the attacks one at a time. This allows us to concentrate on one point of attack without outside concerns distracting us. When the first attack has been executed, one moves to the second attack and so on. The input and output attacks are described in the sections that follow, organized according to the four capabilities that software possesses. Data and computation attacks are presented in the next chapter.

Exploring the Input Domain

One of the main problems in testing is that most applications are written without clear, documented requirements. Testers usually lack good specifications of behavior. This is very unfortunate, but we must test the product anyway. Obviously, this puts us in a tremendously difficult situation: We must test a product whose purpose is unclear (because we lack good requirements) and whose expected behavior is anyone's guess (because there is no written specification).

I encourage every tester to get as much information about behavior as possible. User guides, competing products, and prior versions of the same product are all helpful. However, I am not going to whine about the lack of good specs. This is a fact of life, and other authors have written extensively on ways to get organizations to write and maintain requirements. My purpose is to give you insight into effective testing even when you do not have sufficient documentation.

The most unfortunate thing that a lack of documentation does is leave testers in the dark. Instead of reading about a program's behavior, we must spend time learning the application by using it. Too often, this leaves inexperienced testers banging on the keyboard, hoping that the application breaks.

Inputs need not be applied in such an ad hoc manner. Instead, every applied input should be part of an effective attack or part of exploring the functionality for a plan of attack. In the latter case, testers should *act like a user* to the best of their knowledge of how users will use the application. In other words, testers should apply inputs that force the application to *get real work done*. If you are testing a word processor, then create, format, and edit a document. Put yourself in the user's shoes and do what you think they'll be doing with the application (for example, creating reports, newsletters, correspondence, etc.). Once you understand the functionality sufficiently, it's time to get nasty. Here's my advice on how to accomplish this.

ATTACK 1   Apply inputs that force all error messages to occur

WHEN to apply this attack

The ability to deflect bad input or to appropriately respond to it is an essential characteristic of good software. This first attack tests that software possesses this important capability. Forcing error messages to occur is applicable to nearly every software application ever written. Software should appropriately respond to bad input or it should successfully prevent the input from getting to the software. The only way to know for sure is to test the application with a battery of bad input.

> **Forcing all error messages to occur** will ensure that you test the error code that the developers wrote to handle erroneous input. The idea is to apply inputs that are out of the acceptable range or of the wrong type, so that the error handlers are invoked. Because error code is difficult to get right, you are likely to break the software with this attack.

There are many factors to consider when staging this attack. Perhaps the most important is to consider the tools that developers use to handle bad input. Developers have three techniques at their disposal:

1. *Input filters* can prevent bad input from getting to the software under test. In effect, bad inputs are filtered (by a graphical user interface), and only legal inputs are allowed past the interface.

2. *Input checking* can ensure that the software will not execute using bad input. The simplest case is that every time an input enters the system, the developer inserts an "if" statement to ensure that the input is legal before it is processed (that is, "if" the input is legal "then" process it, "else" display an error message). During this first attack, it is our goal to ensure that we see all such error messages.

3. *Exception handlers* are a last resort and are used to clean up after the software has failed as a result of processing bad input. In other words, bad inputs are allowed into the system, used in processing, and the system is allowed to fail. The exception handler is a routine that is called when the software fails. It usually contains code that resets internal variables, closes files, and restores the ability of the software to interact with its users. In general, some error messages are also displayed.

Testers must consider each input that the software under test accepts. They must focus on erroneous values. The idea is to enter values that are too big, too small, too long, or too short (that is, values that are out of the acceptable range or values of the wrong data type).

Don't go overboard though. Future attacks will round out the completeness of your tests. This first attack should ensure that you see each error message that the application can generate *at least once*. Once you've seen a message, move on to another one.

WHAT software faults make this attack successful?

The reason this is an effective attack is that error cases require developers to write additional error-checking code. Writing such conditions often means that the developer has to stop thinking about the main-line functional code and consider erroneous data. This redirection of design activity is often done sloppily. Worse, many developers postpone writing the error code and never get back to it.

It's amazingly difficult to make a program fail gracefully, and such difficulty usually means bugs. Some error messages are no-brainers. Simply pause execution to display the message and continue to the next input or when a timer expires. However, other error messages result from an exception being thrown and an exception handler being executed. Exception handlers (or any centralized error routine) are problematic because the instruction pointer changes abruptly without creating corresponding changes to the data state. Suddenly, the exception handler is executing, and all kinds of data problems can ensue: Files could still be open, memory could still be allocated, and data structures could contain values that are no longer useful. When control returns to the main routine, it is hard to say at what point the error handler got called and what side effects might be waiting to trip up unwary developers. Opening a file could fail because the file might already be open, or you might use data structures without realizing what data is contained in them. If we ensure that we've seen all error messages and the system still works well, we've done a huge service to our users (not to mention to our maintenance developers).

HOW to determine if this attack exposes failures

The major defect one will find with this attack is missing error cases: input data that the developer did not know was erroneous or individual cases that were overlooked. Missing cases usually cause the software to hang or crash.

One should also be on the lookout for misplaced error messages. Sometimes the developer gets the error message right but assigns it to the wrong input values. Thus the message seems like nonsense for the input values submitted.

Finally, of pure nuisance value are uninformative error messages. Although such messages cause no direct harm to the user, they are sloppy and will cast doubt in a user's mind on the credibility of the software producer. "Error 5 – Unknown Data" might have seemed like a good idea to a developer, but it will cause confusion in the mind of the user, who will have no idea what he did wrong.

HOW to conduct this attack

Whether one is testing an input field in a GUI panel or a parameter in an API call, one must consider *properties* of an input when conducting this attack. Some general properties to consider are the following:

1. *Input type:* Entering invalid types will often cause an error message. For example, if the input in question is an integer, enter a real number or a character.

2. *Input length:* For character (alphanumeric) inputs, entering too many characters will often elicit an error message.

3. *Boundary values:* Every numeric data type has boundary values, and sometimes these values represent special cases. The integer zero, for example, is the boundary between positive and negative numbers.

For example, exceeding boundary values shows an interesting bug in Microsoft Word® 2000 (shown in Fig. 2.1) in which an error message appears twice in a row for no reason. Certainly, this is not a devastating error on the part of the developers, but it is very annoying (perhaps even insulting) to the user because no one likes to be reminded of his mistakes. To reproduce this behavior, launch Word®, choose the "Insert" menu and select the "Index and Tables" tab. Change the "Column" field to five and press the enter key. Note that since the maximum boundary is four, this action will cause the application to correctly display an error message. However, the message appears twice to annoy, inconvenience, and perhaps insult the user.

FIGURE 2.1

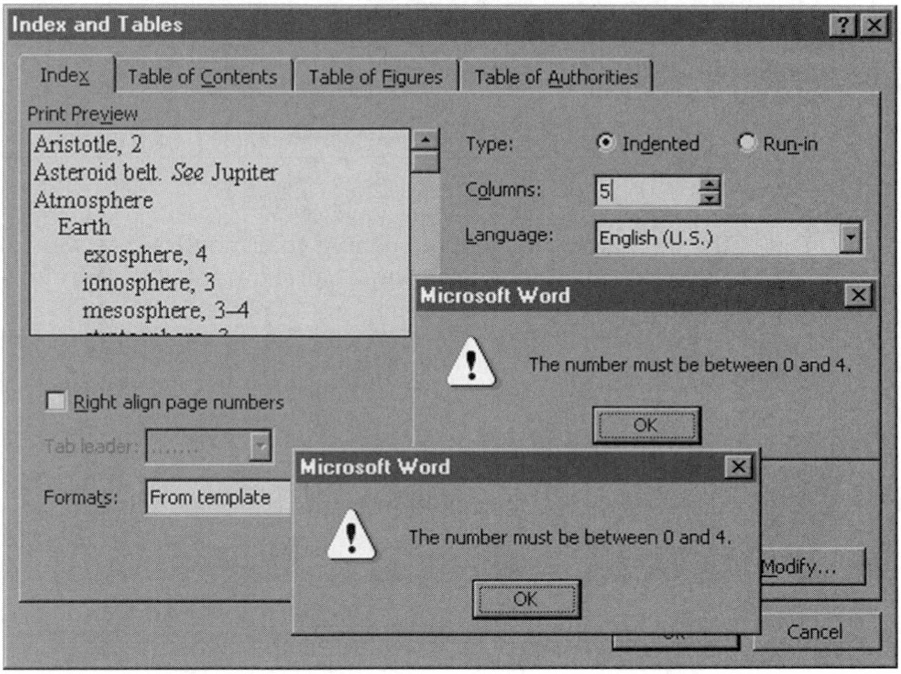

When performing this attack you may find beauties like Fig. 2.2 (reproducible on Windows ME and PowerPoint 2000 by inserting a MSVSA Button Class Object from the "Insert" menu, "Object" item).

FIGURE 2.2

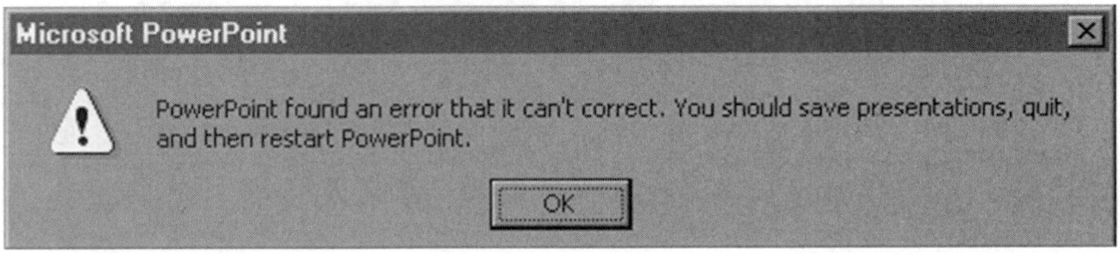

My favorite error message of all time is shown in Fig. 2.3.

FIGURE 2.3

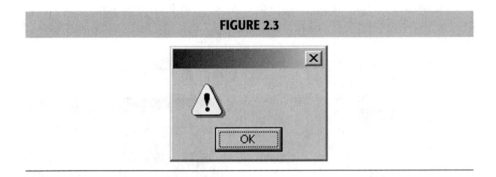

This is the software equivalent of opening your mouth to say something important and then not remembering what you wanted to say. Phrased in the immortal words of Homer Simpson: "Doh!"

For your reference, Table 2.1 shows the boundary values of some common data types.

TABLE 2.1

Type	Length	Range
Unsigned integer	2 bytes	0 to 65,535
	4 bytes	0 to 4,294,967,295
Signed integer	2 bytes	-32,768 to 32,767
	4 bytes	-2,147,483,648 to 2,147,483,647
Character	1 byte	256 different values
	2 bytes	65,535 different values
Boolean	1 byte	True or False
Floating point number	4 bytes	1.2e-38 to 3.4e+38
	8 bytes	2.2e-308 to 1.8e+308
	10 bytes	3.4e4932 to 1.1e+4932

ATTACK 2   Apply inputs that force the software to establish default values

WHEN to apply this attack

Whenever variables are used in software, they must be assigned a legitimate value. If they are used before a legitimate value has been assigned, the software will fail. The correct sequence of operations is as follows:

Variable is declared ⟶ Variable is assigned a value ⟶ Variable is used

> **Forcing the software to establish or use default values** will ensure that the widest variety of default values for internal data items is tested. The idea is to force the software to establish or use data that may not have been initialized with a suitable default value. If developers failed to initialize data, the software will break when that data is used.

However, it is often the case that the middle step—the assignment of a value—is inadvertently skipped. Because product managers and developers have overlapping responsibility to determine what appropriate default values should be, there is often confusion about whether all such values have been determined.

Another, more straightforward context is simply that a default value is assigned and the users consider it a nonoptimal value. Certainly, this is not a crashing-failure scenario, but it can be an inconvenient feature for users to work around.

This attack tests for all such cases and is applicable for any program that declares, initializes, and uses data. Testers must be able to identify such data and determine how it is used in assignment statements, computation, and communication with other program components. This attack is not applicable to other types of data modification that are not directly related to originally assigned default values (we'll cover these attacks in the next chapter).

WHAT software faults make this attack successful?

Although many uninitialized default value cases can be caught at compile time using the right compiler settings or code-analysis tools, there are cases in which this fault can propagate to release. Sometimes developers simply forget to use such tools, or one or both of the following situations occur.

The omission of variable initialization is often the result of the lack of user input. Because the user may choose to leave an input field blank, the software under test may inadvertently accept the input and use the variable without having a value assigned. Obviously, the fix to this problem is to ensure that every variable used has been assigned a *default value* so that the situation never arises.

Of course, code that establishes the default and other code that manipulates the value could also be out of sync. The most common example of this is that in one case the value starts at zero and in another case the value starts at one.

HOW to determine if this attack exposes failures

Sometimes the use of an uninitialized variable causes a general protection violation, and the application crashes. Obviously, this is an easy situation for testers to detect. However, a worse case is that the compiler uses a random memory location as the value of the variable in question. In such a case, the use of the variable might actually work (in that the software won't crash), but a wrong result will be produced. Testers must closely analyze the output of the software in question, looking for things like garbage characters, too many values in a list of data values, too few items, wrong data types being displayed or returned (for example, a character showing up where you expect only numbers), and so forth. Exact quantification of how this fault will manifest is not feasible. Testers must use their own discretion in oracle design.

Testers should also question each default value that the software displays. Is it the right value? Will users appreciate not having to retype the value, or will they change it often enough to make it a hassle?

HOW to conduct this attack

Here are some general guidelines for identifying data that is used in a software application:

1. Look for option buttons, configuration panels, setup screens, and so forth. The data that is displayed on such screens is often used in many places throughout the application.

2. Be mindful of the data that you are inputting into the software and consider ways in which you believe the data is being used.

3. Consult the source code (if available) for data declaration sections.

Once the data is identified, here are some things one can do to the data to force it to use (or misuse) assigned default values.

1.   Accept default values that the software displays. Sometimes the soft-
     ware is counting on the user to enter a value. If you don't enter any,
     the software may fail. You can accomplish this by simply pressing
     "OK".

2.   Enter null values. If a value is displayed, delete it.

3.   Change a default value to another acceptable value, and change it back
     again. This makes the software forget its default and work from a dif-
     ferent context of initial data values. In other words, once the data has a
     value, it may react differently than it did when the value was assigned
     for the first time.

4.   Enter a legitimate value, and change it back to a null value. This uses
     the same reasoning as the previous point.

I love this attack because often it means doing nothing. Just click "OK" and
watch the application die. Why would something so simple constitute an
effective attack? Just because the tester did nothing does not mean the software doesn't have to work. In fact, establishing defaults is a fairly intricate
programming task. Developers have to make sure that variables are initialized before a loop is entered or before a function call is made. If this does-
n't happen, often an internal variable is used without being initialized. The
result is often catastrophic.

For example, in Word 2000 the dialog seen in Fig. 2.4 has an options
menu that, when left unchanged, actually makes controls disappear when
the dialog is redisplayed. Compare the dialog on the left with the one on
the right. Notice any missing controls? Moreover, it changes the display
from three headings to nine headings without the user entering any values!
To reproduce this behavior, select the "Insert" menu and choose the "Index
and Tables" item. Click the "Table of Contents" tab, click the "Options"
button, and press Enter.

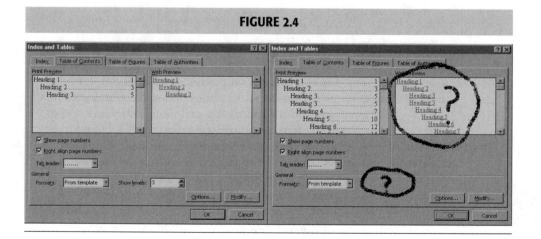

FIGURE 2.4

This odd behavior nicely demonstrates the second attack—force software to display the value of internal data and change some (but not all) or none of the values. This requires defaults to be set; if no defaults have been coded, the software may very well fail.

Sometimes forcing defaults requires changing values from their initial settings and changing them a second time to an improper configuration. These back-to-back changes ensure that the default settings can be reestablished once they are changed to other valid values.

ATTACK 3   Explore allowable character sets and data types

WHEN to apply this attack

Whenever an application accepts strings as input, a question arises: Which characters does the application treat as special cases? Testing these special case values is a good way to find bugs.

> **Exploring the allowable character sets and data types** will test for cases in which the developers failed to write error-handling code. Enter reserved keywords from the OS or underlying programming languages and swap from ASCII to UNICODE fonts. If the developers used outdated APIs or failed to consider such special characters, the software will break.

There are several factors that affect the answer:

1. *Character sets* usually have ordinary members and special members. For example, the ASCII character set possesses ordinary alphanumeric characters and special characters like control characters and symbols. Applications can sometimes handle only ordinary characters and get confused when special characters are input. The UNICODE character set represents an even greater challenge because it is less familiar and has many more possible characters to consider.

2. *Programming languages* in which our applications are implemented often have specific ways of treating certain characters and character strings. C, for example, uses strings like \n, ++, and & for very specific purposes. If these strings are entered into a dialog box, they may be misinterpreted. Their special meaning often demands special

handling. Furthermore, programming languages often confuse spaces and quotation marks, particularly when either of these is embedded inside a pair of quotation marks.

3.　*Operating systems* on which our applications execute also have a set of reserved strings for device names, system objects, and programs. Whenever these names are used inside a program, strange failures may occur.

It is very wise to learn as much as you can about character sets, programming languages, and operating systems when it comes to reserved strings and their special consideration.

For your reference, Table 2.2 defines the ASCII character set and some values that might be troublesome, depending on your application and operating environment. This table is derived from work by my student Scott Chase, and it is reprinted in a modified form with his permission.

TABLE 2.2				
Character Values	**ASCII Values**	**Applicability**	**Use**	**Fault Model**
NUL (^@)	0	O/S; Windows	MS-DOS uses NUL-terminated strings in system functions.	Embedded nulls may affect strings used for system calls. NUL may cause all characters after to be ignored.
		O/S; UNIX	UNIX uses NUL-terminated strings for all system functions.	Embedded nulls may affect strings used for system calls. NUL may cause all characters after to be ignored.
		Language; C, C++, and others	C and C++ use NUL as the string-termination character for all standard library functions.	Embedded nulls may affect any string input field. NUL may cause all characters after to be ignored.
ETX (^C)	3	Shell; Windows	MS-DOS uses ETX as the program-interrupt character.	Program may interrupt upon input of ETX.
		Shell; UNIX	UNIX shells use ETX as the program-interrupt character.	Program may interrupt upon input of ETX.
EOT (^D)	4	O/S; UNIX	UNIX uses EOT as the text end-of-file character.	EOT may have a wide range of effects in input strings; characters after input may be ignored; input or program may terminate, or unpredictable behavior might occur.
		Shell; UNIX	Many UNIX shells use EOT as the end-of-transmission character.	EOT may cause the application or shell to terminate.

TABLE 2.2 *(Cont.)*				
Character Values	**ASCII Values**	**Applicability**	**Use**	**Fault Model**
SOH, ENQ, ACK, VT, SO, SI, DLE, DC2, DC4, NAK, SYN, ETB, EM, FS, GS, RS, US	*various*	All	Miscellaneous nonprinting characters.	Legacy characters from teletypes with no fixed modern use. May be used as sentinel values in strings. May cause emission of non-ASCII character.
BEL (^G)	7	All	Audible bell character.	May cause the audible bell to ring during input or output of the string; may leave an embedded bell character in persistent data.
BS (^H)	8	O/S; Windows	Backspace.	May cause backspace to be embedded in persistent data. May cause backspacing or cursor movement without visible effect.
		Shell; UNIX	Backspace.	Some shells and applications use BS as the backspace character, while others use DEL. May cause persistent data and display problems.
TAB (^I)	9	All	Horizontal Tab.	Tab key may be expanded as unintentional spaces in persistent data, or it may remain a TAB character when it should be expanded.
LF (^J)	10	O/S; Windows	Linefeed.	Windows uses CR/LF as a linespace character. Extra LFs may cause persistent data problems.
		O/S; UNIX	Linefeed.	LF is used as a linespace character. May embed unintentional linespaces.
			Linefeed.	UNIX uses LF as the linespace, and Windows uses CR/LF. Many possible problems.

TABLE 2.2 *(Cont.)*				
Character Values	**ASCII Values**	**Applicability**	**Use**	**Fault Model**
FF (^L)	12	Shell; UNIX	Formfeed.	May cause scrolling or other problems in some shells.
		All	Formfeed.	May cause display and especially printing problems with persistent data if embedded.
CR (^M)	13	All	*See LF.*	
		All	Carriage Return.	May cause functions assigned CTRL-M to be unachievable.
DC1, DC3 (^Q, ^S)	17, 19	Shell; UNIX	XON/XOFF.	Terminal handshaking characters. DC3 may cause input echo to freeze, looking like a lockup. DC1 may not perform its assigned function, instead transmitting the XON signal.
CAN (^X)	24	Shell; Windows	Causes previous text to be canceled and new input to be taken.	May cause previous inputs to be ignored.
		Shell; UNIX	Causes previous text to be canceled.	May cause previous inputs to be ignored.
SUB (^Z)	26	O/S; Windows	Text end-of-file character.	SUB may have a wide range of effects in input strings; characters after input may be ignored; input or program may terminate, or unpredictable behavior might occur.
		Shell; UNIX	Shell escape character; SUB is used to suspend the running program and escape to the shell.	May cause program execution to be suspended.
SPACE	32	Shell; UNIX	Space is used to delimit arguments in some programs.	Embedded spaces may have undesirable effects if the string is to be later treated as an argument.
!	33	Shell; UNIX	Used to expand a history command in some shells.	The "!" may be expanded when used as part of a shell command.

				TABLE 2.2 (Cont.)	

Character Values	ASCII Values	Applicability	Use	Fault Model
"	34	Language; C, C++, VB, and others	Quotations are used to delimit strings in many languages.	Mismatched quotes, embedded quotes, etc. may cause undesirable behavior if the strings are later interpreted or processed.
# ( ) , - . / @ [ ] : ; = ^ _ { } ~	Various		No known side effects.	
$	36	Shell; UNIX	The "$" is used as the environment expansion character.	May expand the token with its environment variable value. *(e.g., $1.00 might expand to <value of argument-1>.0.*
%	37	Shell; Windows	The "%" is used as the environment expansion character.	May expand the token with its environment variable value. *(e.g., 10%20% might expand to 10<value of variable "20">.*
		Language; C, C++	The "%" character is used as the argument expansion character in certain string functions.	May cause crashes, data corruption, and other problems if "%" is interpreted to mean a function argument expansion in a string.
&	38	Shell; UNIX	Suspend character; causes shell invocation to run in background.	May cause background running of shell commands with accompanying timing and security problems.
'	39	Language; Pascal; Fortran; Ada and others	*See ".*	
*	42	Shell; Windows; UNIX	Wildcard character.	May expand in unpredictable ways if interpreted.
+	43	Shell; UNIX	Regular expression character.	May expand in unpredictable ways if interpreted.
<, >, |	60, 62, 124	Shell; UNIX; Windows	Redirection characters; in certain shells, input can be directed to and from files.	May produce unpredictable results and cause security problems.
?	63	Shell; UNIX	Regular expression character.	May expand in unpredictable ways if interpreted.

TABLE 2.2 *(Cont.)*				
Character Values	**ASCII Values**	**Applicability**	**Use**	**Fault Model**
0–9	48–57		Numbers.	
A–Z	65–90		Uppercase letters.	
\	92	Language; C, C++	Escape character; used to embed nonconforming characters in strings.	May have any number of unusual effects if the string is expanded or interpreted; \000 and \0 produce NUL, \n the newline, \a bell, etc.
a–z	97–122		Lowercase letters.	
DEL	127	Shell; UNIX	*See BS.*	

WHAT software faults make this attack successful?

Some input values require special handling when they are read as input. Handling erroneous input is an obvious example. However, many other inputs may require special handling. If the developer failed to consider any of these special circumstances, these inputs may cause the program to fail.

HOW to determine if this attack exposes failures

When software is not specifically programmed to handle special inputs, they are often treated as the "otherwise" case (for example, the default branch of a case/switch statement). The tester must be aware of default behavior and watch for it. If the developer left off the default case, the software may hang. In my experience, software rarely crashes outright due to this attack, but it can hang so that a tester's only recourse is to kill its process (for example, using the Task Manager in Windows).

Because this attack deals with characters and strings, another possibility is that the application will incorrectly render a string. Testers must carefully analyze generated strings to ensure they contain no unwanted characters.

HOW to conduct this attack

It is helpful to make reference tables for your application to guide you in planning and conducting this attack. Document information about the underlying operating system, programming language, character set, and so forth that will allow your team to make good decisions about which characters and data types to apply as input.

Fig. 2.5 shows such a case, using a special device name as a file name. The application simply hangs without warning. To reproduce this behavior in Microsoft Internet Explorer® version 5.5, type "file://c:\AUX" in the URL field and press Enter.

FIGURE 2.5

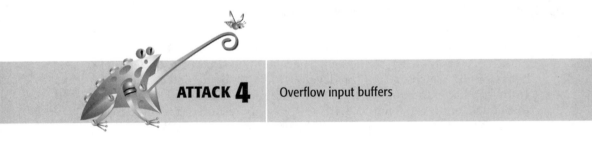

ATTACK 4   Overflow input buffers

WHEN to apply this attack

Another string-based attack is the ubiquitous buffer overflow. The idea here is to enter long strings to overflow input buffers. This is a favorite attack of hackers because sometimes the application is still executing a

> **Overflowing input buffers** serves to find places where there are no constraints on the length of the inputs that the software accepts. Overly long strings can crash the software when handled improperly, so it is important to check each input field for this vulnerability.

process after it crashes. If a hacker attaches an executable string to the end of the long input string, the process may execute it.

This attack is applicable whenever an application allows alphanumeric input, either through GUI controls like text boxes or through parameters of an API call.

WHAT software faults make this attack successful?

The cause of this bug is that developers fail to consider the size of the string that they are passing to in-memory buffers. If the buffer can only hold a fixed-size string and a longer one is passed to it, other memory locations will be overwritten.

HOW to determine if this attack exposes failures

Such illegal activity usually causes the operating system to terminate forcibly the application. So you just have to wait for the software to crash or fail to respond.

HOW to conduct this attack

The first thing to do once an input field is identified is to explore its string-length properties. Ascertain the maximum string length that is sensible and enter longer strings until you get an error message and cannot physically increase the size (in which case the application is doing its job, and there is no bug) or you crash the application by exceeding the allowable length.

Many testers find the following string helpful: type 1234567890, then use the "Copy/Paste" function to increase its size by ten characters each time (for example, 12345678901234567890 and 123456789012345678901234567890, etc.). Using such numbers makes it easy to keep track of the length of the string that causes the failure. Using "Copy/Paste" means that you don't have to retype the string each time you want to apply this attack.

A buffer overflow in Word 2000 is one such exploitable bug. The bug is in the "Find/Replace" feature and is shown in Fig. 2.6. It is interesting that

---

FIGURE 2.6

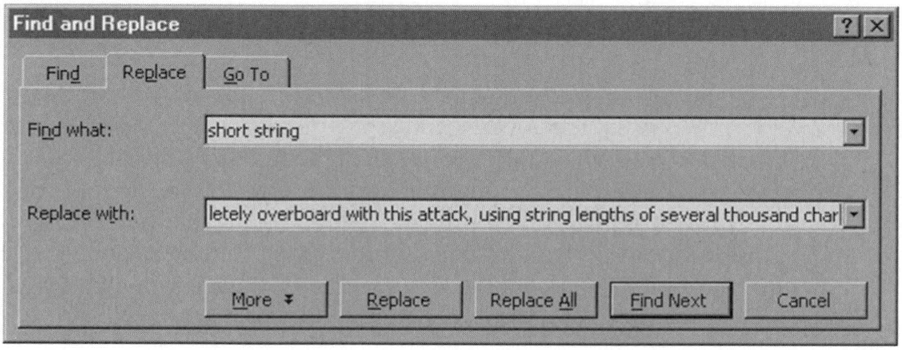

Find and Replace	? X

Find | Replace | Go To

Find what: |short string

Replace with: |letely overboard with this attack, using string lengths of several thousand char

More ≯ | Replace | Replace All | Find Next | Cancel

the "Find" field is properly constrained, but the "Replace" field is not. To reproduce this behavior, choose the "Replace" item from the "Edit" menu. Type anything into the "Find what" field, and type a string of length 256 characters in the "Replace with" field.

This bug in Word requires more than two hundred characters, but it represents a serious concern because users often cut and paste text into the "Find/Replace" dialog. Considering that the ensuing crash will wipe out any unsaved data makes this a "feature" that many users will not appreciate.

In Windows 9x, the crash screen looks like Fig. 2.7:

FIGURE 2.7

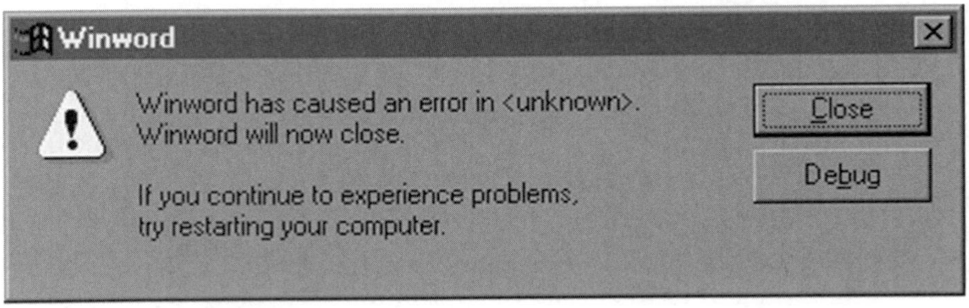

In the Windows NT family, it looks like Fig. 2.8:

FIGURE 2.8

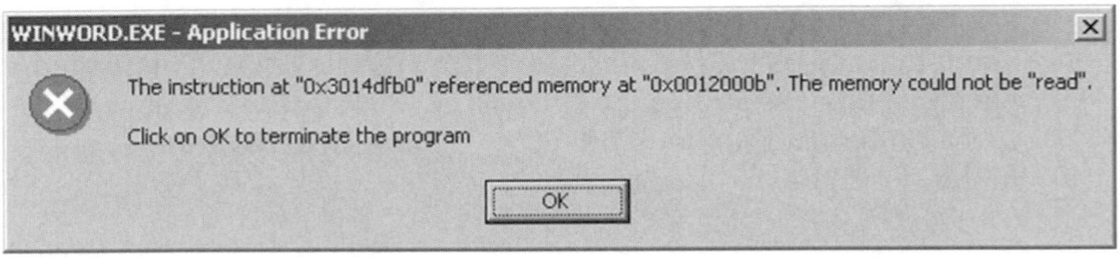

Either way, these screens should become a familiar sight after applying this attack.

Security concerns top the list of reasons why testers should take buffer overruns seriously. However, I notice that novice testers often go completely overboard with this attack, using string lengths of several thousand characters. I often have to rein in my students who love long-string attacks and force them to try something else. The reason is that many developers feel they are low-probability events and will not fix them when the string lengths become outrageous. So it is good to discuss reasonable lengths for input fields with developers before you perform this attack.

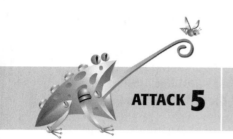

ATTACK 5   Find inputs that may interact and test combinations of their values

<u>WHEN</u> to apply this attack

Up to now, we have only dealt with attacks that exploit a single input entry point in the software. In other words, pick an input location and poke it until the software breaks. This attack deals with multiple inputs that are processed together or that influence one another. The focus is on testing value combinations in which each value has been tested but whose combination of values may cause the software to fail.

For example, an API that can be called with two parameters requires a selection of values for one parameter based on the value of the other parameter. Likewise, a GUI with multiple input fields on a single panel may contain related inputs. Often the combination of values was programmed incorrectly because of the complexity of the logic involved in checking their values.

Because exhaustive testing of all input combinations is infeasible, it is important to use this attack to select a good subset from the set of possible combinations. Suppose, for example, an input panel contains fields for two unsigned two-byte integers. Each field can assume one of 65,535 values, meaning that the two fields combined have $65,535^2$ value combinations.

The sheer numbers involved make deploying this attack daunting. It is therefore important that testers identify fields that really have a relationship. I will reveal tips for accomplishing this and give a concrete example.

<u>WHAT</u> software faults make this attack successful?

Just as testers can overlook the relationship between two input variables, so can developers, particularly when multiple developers are working on a common code base.

> **Testing input combinations** will find subtle but damaging bugs that are due to the values of multiple input fields. Whereas other input attacks focus on a single input, the idea here is to choose values for several input fields so that input relationships are tested. Coding error cases for such multiple-value relationships is difficult, and testing that it was done properly is very important.

Moreover, the programming logic required to check a single value of a variable is relatively straightforward. However, when multiple variables must be checked, more complex control structures are required. A developer may have to write a multilevel-nested "if" statement to check multiple related values. Such control structures are hard to think through and to debug. They are even harder to maintain if they must be changed, either for a bug fix or to add new functionality.

Code changes can also add new constraints to existing variables. These new constraints may affect input relationships in many unpredictable ways, either adding new relationships or modifying existing ones. Obviously, keeping on top of all this is problematic for developers.

HOW to determine if this attack exposes failures

Because inputs are stored internally and used in computation, these faults can cause the software to process incorrect inputs. The result can be that corrupt data is stored or used to produce an output. Testers must determine how the software uses the input and track the effect of the input as the software executes.

Testers should watch for incorrect outputs and obvious signs of data corruption (for example, failure to redraw a screen or garbled displays). Finally, incorrect inputs can sometimes cause the software to crash.

HOW to conduct this attack

The first step in deploying this attack is to identify candidate variables and explore their relationship. Variables can be considered "relatives" if they possess either of the following properties:

1. They describe aspects of a common internal data structure. Testers should consider both the properties and the content (that is, values that get stored) of the data structure. For example, an input panel that requests the user to enter the "size" and "dimensions" of a list indicates to the tester that he is being asked to supply properties (for example, size and dimension) of a single internal data structure (for example, the list).

2. They are used together in an internal computation. Sometimes inputs are related because they are used as operands in an internal computation. This can be a single computation or a series of computations that use related data. For example, if a word processor takes the left, right, upper, and lower margin as input, one would expect that these values would be used together to compute the page size.

Selecting single values to apply often means selecting values at the extreme range of acceptable values, such as very small or very large integers. When multiple input fields are considered, specific tests include using a large value for one input and a small value for another.

Once you have determined which inputs are related or independent—and defined the value combinations you want to test—you may consider using a tool like Telcordia's AETG (http://aetgweb.argreenhouse.com) to generate the minimal set of combinations that can be run to give coverage, based on aspects of statistical design of experiments.

For example, try the following with Word 2000. Choose the "Insert" option from the "Table" menu and experiment with the allowable values for the number of columns and rows. You will soon realize that these input fields cannot be overflowed. You will also see that the maximum number of columns is sixty-three and the maximum number of rows is 32,767. This is a good example of input-value dependence. If you enter small numbers for both fields, Word handles it just fine. A large number for one and a small number for the other is also fine. But if you enter a value above fifty for the columns and above 32,000 for the rows, the application hangs because it overwhelms the machine's CPU cycles. Be careful to save your work first.

Which combinations are problematic? This issue is being actively researched, but an approach we have found to be especially effective is to determine an output you want to generate and find input combinations that cause the output to occur. If the outcome you want is a crash, entering large numbers is a good approach.

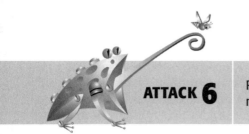

ATTACK 6   Repeat the same input or series of inputs numerous times

WHEN to apply this attack

This attack is applicable under any circumstance in which an application accepts input inside a loop. In other words, the application receives input, processes it, and waits until the user enters another input. The idea behind this attack is to enter a single input, or a series of inputs, over and over.

> **Repeating the same input numerous times** will consume resources and cause data initialization problems. Just because something worked once does not mean it will work twice; sometimes the first input will cause a value to be set internally that will break the software when the input is reapplied.

WHAT software faults make this attack successful?

Repetition has the effect of gobbling resources and stressing an application's stored data space, not to mention uncovering undesirable side effects. Unfortunately, most applications are unaware of their own space and time limitations, and many developers assume that plenty of resources are always available. The fault that developers create is the failure to properly monitor memory and data usage when directed to perform a series of operations over and over.

Another fault you'll uncover with this attack deals with the assumptions that developers make about default values. The first time you apply an input generally means you are working with internal default values (of data structures) that the developer intended you to use. Subsequent applications of the same input may result in different default values being used. If the developer failed to consider these defaults, the input may make the software fail.

HOW to determine if this attack exposes failures

Because this attack stresses memory usage, the result can be unpredictable. However, for GUI applications, watch for misplaced screen refreshing (either too often or, more likely, not often enough). Another common manifestation is that the machine will bog down in the repetitive tasks and become unresponsive, taking way too much time to complete simple tasks.

Consider also the use of a memory-leak detector. Because this attack will cause the same function to be executed many times, memory leaks may become a problem if they are present. Without such a tool, you will have to be patient to detect the resulting performance degradation without automated assistance.

HOW to conduct this attack

The general design of this attack is to select an input, or a series of inputs, and apply it over and over until you reach an internally programmed limit or you find a failure. The key is in selecting the right input sequence.

The first inputs that become obvious candidates are those that you *expect* the user to apply numerous times. For example, it is natural to assume that a user of a math package will insert many matching pairs of parentheses into an equation. One might expect a user to repeat text-formatting inputs for every paragraph in a word processor or download a number of Web pages one after another. Inputs or input sequences that a user is likely to apply are certainly ones we want to test.

Next, testers should consider how inputs are used internally. If it is obvious that a set of inputs requires a great deal of memory or processing time, which is usually observable by looking for situations in which the application slows down, then repeated application of the same inputs will serve to stress memory and speed.

An example of this is the equation editor for Word, which seems to be unaware that it can handle only ten levels of nested brackets. Indeed, after the tenth pair of brackets, the equation disappears. To reproduce this behavior, select the "Insert" menu and choose the "Object" item. From the "Object type" list box, choose "Microsoft Equation 3.0." This editor allows you to insert nested brackets. Insert ten sets, and you will get the error message seen in Fig. 2.9.

FIGURE 2.9

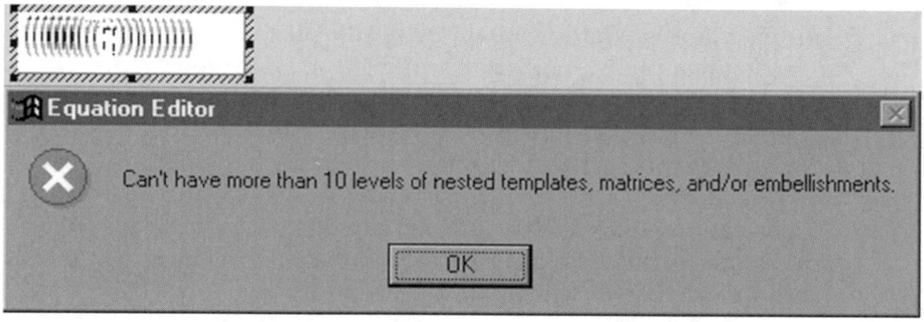

Accept the message and type any equation inside the innermost brackets, as seen in Fig. 2.10.

FIGURE 2.10

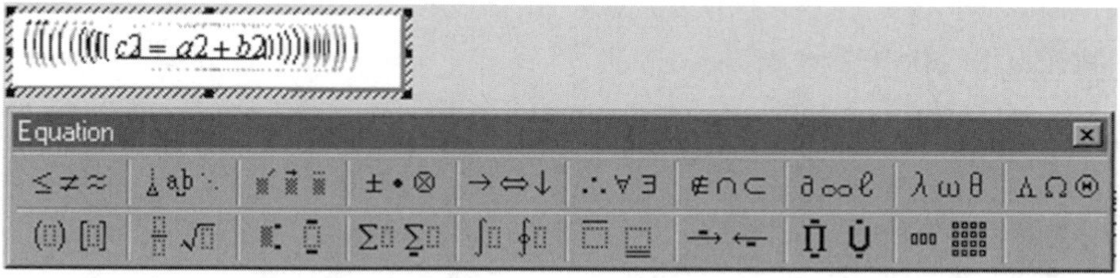

Finally, insert one more pair of brackets, and the message again appears. Accept the message, and the equation disappears. Try as you might, you cannot get it to come back again (see Fig. 2.11).

FIGURE 2.11

Exploring Outputs

Applying inputs is fairly straightforward. Unfortunately, many testers equate testing with applying many different input combinations. However, our research indicates that many bugs are simply too difficult to find by concentrating on inputs alone. Instead, we take the harder approach of beginning with software outputs and working our way back to causal inputs.

Thus the next series of attacks requires us to identify interesting outputs and figure out which inputs are capable of driving the application to generate those outputs. The next set of attacks lends insight into how we select the outputs on which to concentrate.

ATTACK 7   Force different outputs to be generated for each input

WHEN to apply this attack

Context is important for many inputs that we test. Applying the same input in a variety of contexts will ensure that the software works for the most common scenarios and other possible situations of use. This attack

> **Forcing different outputs to be generated for each input** will ensure that testing has uncovered all major behaviors associated with each input. This attack gives testers a framework for thinking through these behaviors and ensuring that testing covers them.

helps a tester determine which contexts must be staged so that an input can be applied in situations that might cause the software to fail.

The idea behind this attack is to determine the possible behavior that the software under test can generate when the user applies a specific input. If one input causes different outputs depending on prior inputs, then testers should ensure that they test each input under a variety of circumstances, ensuring that each output is seen during test.

To apply this attack, testers must have domain expertise or access to written documentation that describes how inputs cause specific behaviors. Without such knowledge or documentation, deploying this attack may be very time consuming.

WHAT software faults make this attack successful?

 Some inputs cause the same behavior every time they are applied. This is a very simple situation to code and to test. Simply apply the input and verify correct behavior. However, this attack describes the situation in which a single input can cause any number of behaviors, depending on prior inputs or the state of the system under test.

This is a much more complex situation for developers to deal with. They must code functions that access internal variables to determine the state of the system. Then they must branch to the appropriate function that implements the desired output behavior. Obviously, this is more involved than simply receiving an input and generating the corresponding output. Because it is more complex to code, there is a good chance that there are bugs.

HOW to determine if this attack exposes failures

 Setting up this attack means enumerating the outputs that can occur from applying a specific input. Because the list of desirable behaviors is known, verifying that the correct one occurs is fairly straightforward.

Another possibility is that there are behaviors that the developer forgot to consider, and thus the software will be missing functionality that this attack should expose.

HOW to conduct this attack

It is often the case that a single input causes any number of outputs to be generated, depending on the context under which the input is applied. For example, if we test a telephone switch, then one input that must be tested is the switch's ability to correctly process the input (that is, the user picks up the phone). Because there are two major outputs that the switch will generate when this input is applied, we must test them both. Consider first the case that the phone is idle, and the user picks up the receiver: The switch will generate a dial-tone output and send it to the user's phone. Now consider the case in which the phone is ringing: The switch will connect the user with the subscriber who placed the call. Thus we have tested the two major outputs (or behaviors) associated with the user picking up the telephone receiver. (Note that previous attacks should have covered the error cases).

The tester's job is to identify inputs in which context might be important and query the specification, product documentation, or our familiarity with the problem to decide how many possible outputs can result when that input is applied. Once such a list is formed, each of the causal situations must be staged and executed.

Identifying all possible outputs for the most important or frequently used inputs is an important exercise. Ensuring that testing covers these outputs can be hard work, but it will pay off by helping us find important bugs that will irritate our users.

ATTACK 8   Force invalid outputs to be generated

WHEN to apply this attack

This is a very effective attack for testers who really understand their problem domain. You must understand the problem that your software is trying to solve so intimately that you know correct or incorrect answers when you see them. Knowing a problem so well that you can enumerate incorrect answers is much harder than it sounds.

> **Forcing invalid outputs to be generated** will help testers think through special cases of input combinations that can lead to the wrong answer being generated. The idea is to list all possible wrong answers and test to see if varying input parameters can generate such answers.

For example, testers unfamiliar with the leap-year rule will be ineffective at testing a calendar program. To such a tester, the date February 29 is likely to seem reasonable. As a further extreme, imagine a person who has never been in an airplane testing a flight simulator. You get the picture. Familiarity with the correct output goes a long way toward helping one be an effective tester.

Thus *understanding the problem domain* is key to applying this attack. For example, if you are testing a calculator and understand that some functions have a restricted range for their result, then trying to find input value combinations that force those invalid results is a worthwhile effort. If you do not understand mathematics, it is likely that such an endeavor will be a waste of time—you might even interpret an incorrect result as correct.

One must ask, "How will I know if a result is invalid?" Only testers who can answer this question convincingly will apply this attack successfully.

WHAT software faults make this attack successful?

 Just as testers who do not understand the solution domain will have trouble, developers with an incomplete understanding of the solution will have a hard time coding it. Indeed, it is this misunderstanding that creates the faults for which we are looking.

In most cases, the faults are overlooked special cases. Inputs that don't follow the general rule (for example, February has neither thirty nor thirty-one days) must be handled in special ways. When developers fail to code special cases for these inputs, the software will produce incorrect results.

HOW to determine if this attack exposes failures

The hardest part about verifying such test inputs is that the software seldom fails in a spectacular manner. Indeed, this attack usually causes the software to produce a result that looks correct. Certainly, the *type* and *format* of the result is usually consistent with previous results. So for this attack, we need to concentrate on the *value* of the result and question its correctness.

HOW to conduct this attack

Testers need to focus on known bad results and come up with the outputs that might force those results to be computed. This focus on outputs is what differentiates output attacks from the input attacks of the previous section.

Many testers find this output-oriented approach unnatural. Indeed, much of the training involved in selecting test cases encourages testers to isolate aspects of the input domain to determine test input. However, this attack requires analysis of aspects of the *outputs*. Thus testers should learn as much about the underlying problem domain as they can. If you are testing a flight simulator, learn about flying an airplane. If you are testing a weapons system, learn about the physics of trajectories. If you are testing a calculator, brush up on your mathematics. Such expertise will enable you to understand the difference between valid and invalid outputs.

However, even when invalid outputs are enumerated, it can still be difficult to figure out which input combinations can force those outputs to occur. Testers must determine which inputs are involved in computing the output in question and then experiment with input combinations to produce the undesirable result. One key ingredient is often input sequencing. Applying the inputs involved in reverse order, or applying them in a variety of sequences, is often effective.

If you are unable to force the invalid output, it is a good thing. If the undesirable behavior you've identified cannot be forced, you've gained confidence that your software only produces correct answers. By all accounts this is a desirable property of software.

One of my favorite bugs falls into this category (see Fig. 2.12). A Y2K-related bug in Windows NT, which was fixed in service pack 5, allowed the system to display the date February 29, 2001—an invalid output because 2001 is not a leap year. In this case, a tester unfamiliar with the leap-year rule would undoubtedly have missed this bug.

FIGURE 2.12

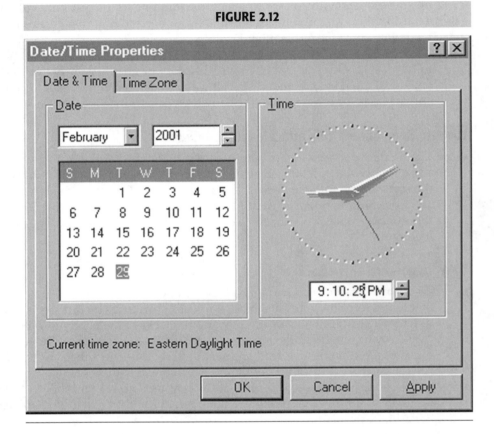

This bug is particularly interesting because simply paging through the calendar will cause it to display the right number of days in February. The behavior is only reproducible when the tester selects February 29 on a valid leap year (for example, 2000). Next, the tester must increment the year by clicking on the associated spin control.

One can see by this example that input sequencing is crucial to isolating the failure. Once the tester identifies February 29, 2001, as the target invalid output, the first step in the causal sequence is to fix the system on the invalid day (for example, February 29) by selecting it on a valid year (for example, 2000). The next step in the sequence, incrementing the year to 2001, completes the attack and exposes the bug. Sequencing of input is the difference in exposing this bug or having it go unnoticed.

| ATTACK **9** | Force properties of an output to change |

WHEN to apply this attack

Some outputs are simple. Send them to the user and forget about them. However, some outputs are editable, changeable, or might otherwise come back to haunt the application under test. Whenever such outputs exist, this attack is applicable.

> **Forcing output properties to change** gives testers a way to think about persistent outputs. Outputs that hang around on the screen or in a file can be updated in ways that cause the software to break. Because internal data can differ between the initial rendering of the output and any subsequent editing of it, the software could work in one case and not the other.

WHAT software faults make this attack successful?

Outputs often have changeable properties associated with them. Perhaps an output has a color, shape, dimension, size, or other attribute that the user can modify. In such situations, the developer must write code that establishes initial or default properties and then write code that will allow the user to edit those same properties. If the code to establish original display characteristics is inconsistent with the code that allows those characteristics to be modified, a problem exists.

Such inconsistencies often come about through code modification. For example, a developer changes code in the initialization routine but fails to make the same change in the modification routine. Remembering to synchronize such code changes is very difficult, especially when the original developer is not the same developer who is making changes.

The reason this attack is often successful has to do with internal data. The first time an output is generated, there is no stored data. However, when the output has been generated once, editing it or one of its properties means that the software must now deal with the established default values.

HOW to determine if this attack exposes failures

Although this attack usually requires painstaking visual screen verification, alert testers can easily spot bugs. The very nature of the attack requires that output properties be identified in advance, so testers are on the lookout for very specific behaviors.

HOW to conduct this attack

The first step is for testers to peruse the outputs that can be generated, looking specifically for those outputs with editable properties. The task thereafter is to force each output to be generated and then edit each of its properties.

The property that is often the most convenient for user interface testing is output size (that is, force display areas to be recomputed by changing the length of inputs and input strings).

A good conceptual example is setting a clock to 9:59 and watching it roll over to 10:00. In the first case the display area is four characters long, and in the second it is five. Going the other way, we establish 12:59 (five characters) and watch the text shrink to 1:00 (four characters). Too often developers write code to work with the initial case of a blank display area, and they are disappointed when the display area already has data in it and new data of different size is used to replace it.

For example, "WordArt" in PowerPoint has an interesting problem. Suppose we enter a long string, as shown in Fig. 2.13.

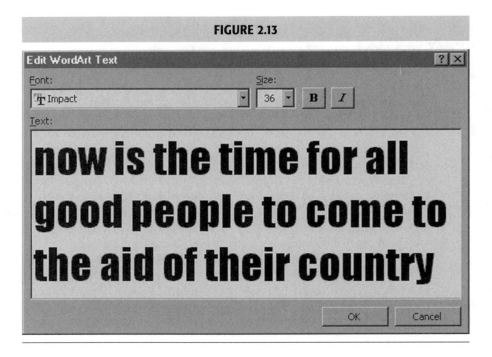

FIGURE 2.13

Notice that the string overlaps the screen boundary because it is too long (see Fig. 2.14).

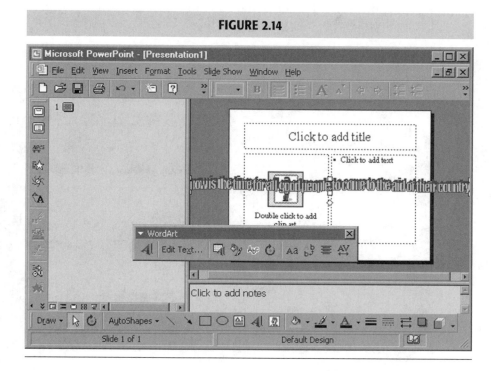

FIGURE 2.14

However, that's not what is really important. Two things went on when the "OK" button was pressed. First, the routine computed the size of the output field needed and populated the field with the text we entered. Now let's edit the string and replace it with a single character (see Fig. 2.15).

FIGURE 2.15

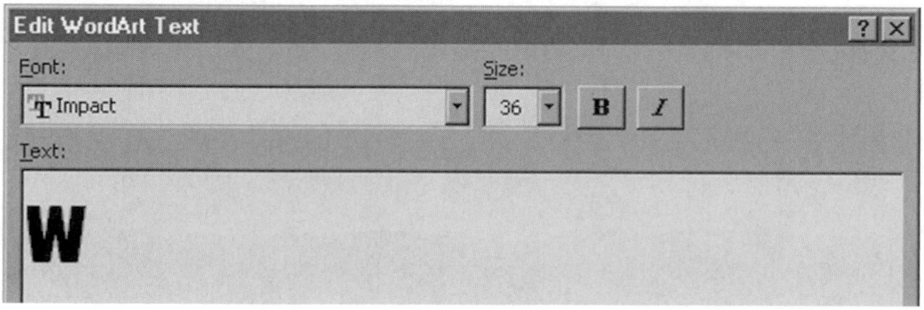

Notice that the display area stays the same size despite the fact that only one character was inserted and the font size was not changed. Thus instead of determining the size of the text box and populating it, which is what happened the first time, the only thing that happened was populating the fixed-size text box (see Fig. 2.16).

FIGURE 2.16

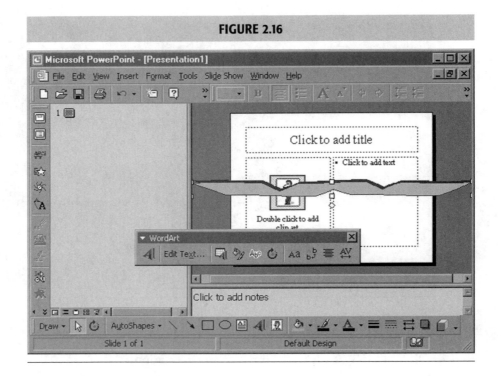

Let's pursue this further. If we edit the string again and type a multiline string, the output is even more interesting (see Fig. 2.17).

This makes it very clear that the text is being crammed into the existing box.

FIGURE 2.17

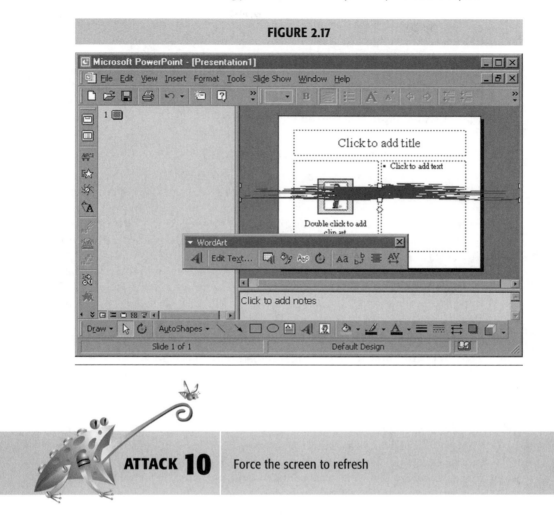

ATTACK 10   Force the screen to refresh

WHEN to apply this attack

This attack is applicable to GUI software in which objects can be written to a window and displayed to the user. Because the very nature of GUIs allows windows to be overlaid, moved, and resized, redrawing or refreshing the screen is commonplace.

> **Forcing the screen to refresh** will help find rendering problems in applications with screen output. The idea is to create and modify objects on the screen so that the application and/or the operating system forces the screen to refresh. The bugs appear when the screen fails to refresh and the displayed objects are garbled.

For all modern GUI platforms, refreshing the screen so that these objects can be redisplayed is problematic. Testing the situations in which the screen is (or should be) forced to refresh will save your users a ton of headaches. Screens that fail to refresh end up looking too cluttered to use properly. This inconvenience to the user, who must figure out how to force a refresh, is so severe that no self-respecting software company should allow known, egregious refresh bugs to ship.

WHAT software faults make this attack successful?

Refreshing the screen or window because you applied input is a major problem for users of modern windows-based GUIs. It is an even bigger problem for developers. Refresh too often, and the application slows. Failing to refresh causes anything from minor annoyances (for example, requiring the user to force refresh) to major bugs (for example, preventing the user from getting work done).

Developers walk a thin tightrope to determine how many refreshes are enough. Sometimes they get it wrong. It is the tester's job to help determine the "sweet spot."

HOW to determine if this attack exposes failures

Like all output attacks, verifying a screen refresh is easy for an alert tester. Although it is difficult to automate, most testers have seen enough desktops to know when one is in need of a good refresh.

HOW to conduct this attack

The general idea in searching for refresh problems is to add, delete, and move objects on the screen. This causes the background object to redisplay. If the redisplay doesn't occur properly and in a timely fashion, you have just found the classic refresh bug.

There are several pieces of advice:

1. It is a good idea to vary the distance you move an object from its original location. Move it a little, then move it a lot. Move it once or twice, then move it a dozen times. This will ensure that you get good coverage of the forced refreshes that the developer could foresee.

2. Overlay objects so only their edges touch. Overlap them a little more until one completely obscures the other. This way you ensure that the refresh isn't dependent on how much or how little of the object needs to be redrawn.

3. Use objects of varying type. If the application supports a specific type of object, use it in carrying out this attack. The mix of text objects, graphic objects, and combination objects can sometimes be problematic.

4. When one object is contained within another object, force the contained object outside the boundaries set by the container object. For example, make the text inside a text-box container too big for the container.

As an example, fire up PowerPoint 2000 and insert a text box on a black page. Type "abc" and the superscript "123." If you change the size of the superscript to a large font (for example, thirty point), the text box does not resize to fit the entire text. Moving the text box around on the screen will cause a nasty refresh problem, as seen in Fig. 2.18.

FIGURE 2.18

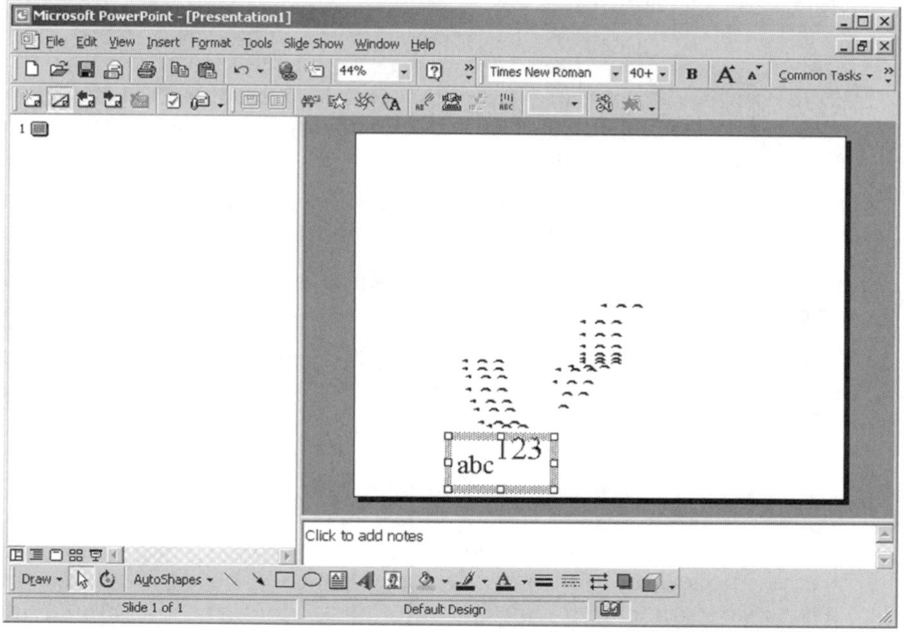

Another recurring refresh problem in Office® 2000 and its competitors is disappearing text. This is most annoying in word processors just around the screen, page, and paragraph formatting boundaries.

Summary of the Input/Output Attacks—A Checklist for Battle

Input Attacks

1. Make sure you see all error messages at least once by applying invalid input. Think of invalid inputs that the developers might have missed.

2. Force the software to assign its default values for any internal variable that can be set through the user interface. First display and accept existing values. Then assign bogus values to force the software to calculate good ones.

3. For every input field, enter values of the wrong type and values that represent strings that may be treated in a special way. Study the OS and programming language and make a list of possible problematic strings. Apply them all in every test entry field.

Summary of the Input/Output Attacks—A Checklist for Battle *(Cont.)*

4. In every input field enter the maximum number of characters allowed.

5. Find input panels where a number of inputs are entered before pressing "OK". Determine legal values for each individual field and try combinations that represent an illegal set of inputs.

6. Find places where inputs are accepted and apply the same input or series of inputs over and over. Choose inputs that cause some underlying computation or data manipulation over inputs that are simply displayed on the screen.

Output Attacks

7. Pick an input, apply it to the software under test, and note the output. Think about other outputs that could occur when this input is applied in other situations. Apply the inputs in these other situations to ensure that each such output is observed during testing.

8. Think of outputs that the software cannot or should not generate. Find a combination or sequence of inputs that will cause one of these illegal outputs to be generated.

9. Apply an input that generates an output with some observable and changeable property, such as size. Force the property to change.

10. Determine when the software under test is refreshing the screen. Create situations where the software refreshes the screen too often or in which it fails to refresh when it should.

■■ Conclusion

Simply going through the attacks in this chapter can exercise a great deal of an application's functionality. Indeed, staging a successful attack usually means experimenting with dozens of possibilities and pursuing a number of dead-ends. However, just because some of this exploration doesn't find bugs does not mean that it is not useful. First, the time spent using the application familiarizes testers with the range of possible functionality and leads to new ideas for additional attacks. Second, successful tests are good news! They indicate that a product is reliable, particularly if those tests are malicious attacks. If code can withstand this treatment, it may very well withstand whatever users can dish out.

Also, never underestimate the value of having a concrete goal in mind when you are testing. I've seen too many testers waste time poking at a keyboard or making random API calls, hoping something breaks. Staging attacks means formulating clear goals—based specifically on things that *could* go wrong—and designing tests to investigate those goals. This way, every test has a purpose, and progress can be readily monitored.

The references at the end of this section contain information about testing techniques and provide good background work on breaking software.

■■ Exercises

Professional testers can use whatever software application they are working on to perform these exercises. Students can choose any application they use frequently. At Florida Tech, we choose an application in advance for our semester-long class and everyone in the class works on it, usually in teams of two.

Once you have selected your application under test, perform the following exercises. Just for fun, we'll refer to the application under test as the "target."

1. Pretend you are a user and use your target application. Think like a real user and use the application to get real work done. While you are doing this make a note of the inputs that you are applying. A good way to organize the inputs is by feature. Make a table of features and list the inputs that can be applied to each one. For example, if you are testing the "Find/Replace" feature of a word processor, your inputs would be <find string>, <replace string>, <ok button>, <cancel button>, and so forth.

2. Apply each of the input attacks to your application. Document the attacks that you applied, the features that worked as specified, and the bugs you found.

3. Use the table you created in Exercise 1 and add a new column to it to document outputs that each feature can generate. Look through the input attacks you ran for Exercise 2 and see how many outputs you generated during those attacks.

4. Apply each of the output attacks to your application. Document the attacks that you applied, the features that worked as specified, and the bugs you found.

5. Make a list of reserved words and symbols for a real operating system. For which attack would you use such a table?

■■ References

1. C. Kaner, J. Faulk, and H. Nguyen, *Testing Computer Software*, New York, Wiley, 1999.

2. B. Beizer, *Black Box Testing Techniques*, Van Nostrand, 1996.

CHAPTER 3

Testing from the User Interface: Data and Computation

Testing Inside the Box

The fault model presented in Chapter 1 provides for black-box-testing (for example, inputs and outputs) and white-box-testing issues (for example, data and computation). However, pure source-code-based white box testing is beyond the scope of this book. Instead, I opt for what is called *gray box testing*, in which abstractions of the code are used as a replacement for having the source available.

This chapter covers attacks that are orchestrated from the user interface but specifically involve internal data and computation. As with the previous chapter, the idea is that testers apply the attacks one at a time. This allows us to concentrate on one point of attack without outside concerns distracting us. When the first attack has been executed, one moves to the second attack and so on.

Exploring Stored Data

Data is the lifeblood of software; if you corrupt it, the software will eventually have to use the bad data, and what happens then may not be pretty. So it is worthwhile to understand how and where data values are established.

Essentially, stored data enters a system by the application reading input and storing it internally or by storing the result of an internal computation. So it is through supplying input and forcing computation that we enable data to flow through the application under test.

However, without access to the source code, many testers do not consider attacks on data. I believe that useful testing can be done even though specifics of the implementation are hidden. I tell my students to practice "looking through the interface." In other words, as you use a software system, take note of what data is being stored. If you enter data on one screen and see it on another, it is being stored. If you detect that information is available when you ask for it, it is being stored.

Some data is easy to see. A table structure in a word processor is one example in which not only the data but the general storage mechanism is displayed on the screen. However, some data is hidden behind the interface and takes analysis to discover its properties.

Once you generally understand the nature of the data being stored, put yourself in the position of the programmer and think of the possible data structures you might use to store such data. The more you know about programming and data structures, the easier it will be to execute the following attacks. The more completely you understand the data you are testing, the more successful these attacks will be at finding bugs.

ATTACK **11**   Apply inputs using a variety of initial conditions

WHEN to apply this attack

Inputs are often applicable in a variety of circumstances. Saving a file, for example, can be performed when changes have been made, and it can also be performed when no changes have been made. Testers are wise to apply each input in many different circumstances to account for the many interactions that users will encounter when using the application. Determining exactly what those circumstances should be is a tricky endeavor, and it is often what separates a really insightful tester from a mediocre one.

> **Applying inputs under a variety of initial conditions** will find problems in which internal data is incompatible with certain inputs and input sequences. Because the logic involved in catching and handling these types of error conditions is complex, it is important that as many inputs as possible be tested independently.

The output-based attack, *force different outputs to be generated for each input*, is related to the current attack. However, in the former attack the concentration focuses on determining the preconditions necessary to generate a specific output. The current attack usually focuses on setting preconditions that cause the application to break by confusing the application.

Thus you should ask, "What preconditions of stored data are likely to make this input not work?"

WHAT software faults make this attack successful?

Whenever computation occurs with inputs and stored data, developers face a challenging situation. They must consider the validity of the input in combination with the validity of the data that may affect the computation. The temptation for developers to check the input without worrying about the variety of internal data is often too sweet to pass up. The result is computation that works only under certain initial conditions of stored data. If those conditions change and the same input is reapplied, the result is often catastrophic for the application under test.

HOW to determine if this attack exposes failures

Unfortunately, verifying correct behavior requires that we consider almost everything for this attack. The best (as far as ease of verification) situation is that the combination of data values and inputs is incompatible and the software crashes when trying to combine them. In the worst scenario, small variations in the output or screen disposition will require painstaking reproductions of the same steps that the software used to arrive at the observed output.

HOW to conduct this attack

Staging this attack requires that we isolate a feature or function to test and consider all possible data objects that are (or could be) used when that feature is executed. Second, we must think about ways to partition the sets of data objects so that each combination in a specific partition will yield roughly the same behavior. When done, the tester must execute one combination from each partition.

Thus you must ask, "Under what circumstances is this particular input likely to be treated differently?" The answer is a list of "circumstances" (that is, initial conditions that must be staged and tested).

An example using the "Group/Ungroup" feature of Word 2000 appears in Fig. 3.1. This feature allows the user to group multiple objects, such as text and graphics, into a single object for easier manipulation. If similar objects are grouped together, the ungroup feature is reliable. However, grouping several bitmap images with a text box causes all kinds of problems when the objects are ungrouped.

In fact, there are really two issues at play here. The fact that there are objects of multiple types grouped together is the main offender, but the failure is easier to see if there is another set of objects that are separately grouped in near proximity to the group in question. As you can see in Fig. 3.1, ungrouping one group causes the second group to be displaced.

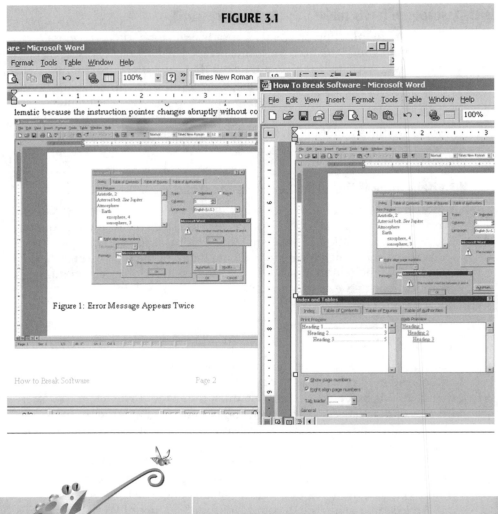

FIGURE 3.1

Figure 1: Error Message Appears Twice

ATTACK 12

Force a data structure to store too many or too few values

WHEN to apply this attack

This attack is mostly applicable in cases in which specific data structures are known. If testers have access to the source code, data structures can be readily obtained. Otherwise, testers will have to identify data structures simply by using the application and second-guessing the developers.

> **Forcing a data structure to store too many or too few values** will ensure that checks on array (and other data structures) boundaries are properly in place. The incorrect coding of these checks can cause underflow or overflow situations and could cause data to be corrupted.

Testers can apply this attack on fixed-sized data structures like arrays. If an array allows a certain number of elements to be stored, it is a candidate for this attack in which testers force the array to store too many or too few values.

The attack can also be applied to data structures that dynamically resize (that is, that grow to fit whatever amount of data a user gives it). Such structures—stacks, queues, lists, and so forth—have an upper boundary that the compiler or operating system defines and limits. Because there is no such thing as an infinite-size structure on finite computers, one can still overflow such structures. The trick is to stay within a size that is reasonably expected to occur during regular use.

This attack finds most of its bugs during unit testing, but some slip through. So system testers should be diligent about applying this attack even though it isn't expected to find many bugs.

WHAT software faults make this attack successful?

Developers often code with respect to a structure's content and forget about the physical limitations (specifically size) of the structure itself. They may write an "AddElement" program that adds a new value to an array. If this program does not account for the end of the array, eventually it will attempt to add an element past the array's upper boundary, and the application will fail. Likewise, a "RemoveElement" program must account for the beginning of the array or risk deleting an item that does not exist.

HOW to determine if this attack exposes failures

Reading or writing beyond array boundaries is usually cause for the operating system to shut down the offending program. Thus testers should watch for crashes. However, memory corruption is not out of the question, so testers should watch for corrupt data and incorrect output caused by using the corrupt data in a computation.

HOW to conduct this attack

There is an upper limit on the size of all data structures. Some data structures can grow to fill the capacity of machine memory or hard disk space, and others have a fixed upper limit. For example, a running monthly sales average might be stored in an array bounded at twelve, one for each month of the year.

If you can detect the limits on a data structure, force too many values into the structure. If the number is particularly large, the developer may have been sloppy and not programmed an error case for overflow. You can accomplish this by applying inputs that add elements to lists of values that are stored internally.

Pay special attention to structures whose limits fall on the boundary of data types 256, 1,024, 32,767, and so on. Such limits are often imposed simply by declaration of the structure's size and very often lack an overflow error case.

Underflow is also a possibility and should be tested. This is easy, requiring only that we delete one more element than we add. Delete when the structure is empty, add an element, delete two elements, and so on. Give up if the application handles three or four attempts.

Earlier we broke Microsoft Word by using the input attack for combining inputs. In that attack we entered large values for the row and column indexes of an inserted table. We also noticed the limit on the number of rows to be 32,767—the upper boundary of a two-byte signed integer.

Applying the current attack on the number of rows will create many very peculiar behaviors, none of which are good news for users. Although the errant behavior is different depending on how much memory your machine has, my favorite outcome is shown in Fig. 3.2.

Go to the "Table" menu and select the "Insert" item. Choose a small value for the number of columns and 32,767 for the number of rows.

Now add rows to overflow this structure. After a dozen or so new rows, move the cursor to the bottom of the table. Note the page count on the status bar located at the bottom of the window. On my machine, the page count grows by one page every half second or so. After a couple of minutes, Word will lock up.

FIGURE 3.2

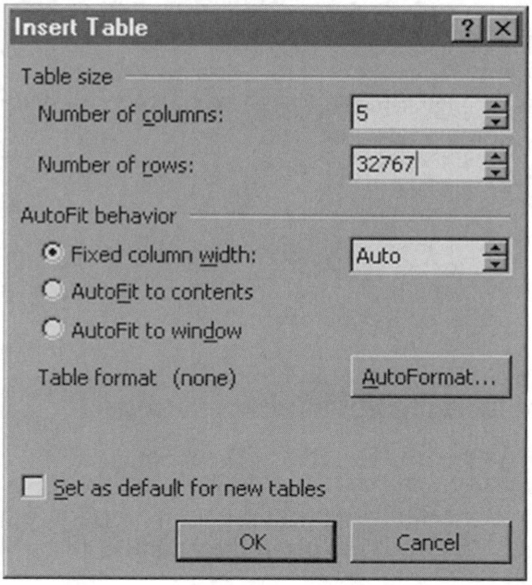

ATTACK 13 Investigate alternative ways to modify internal data constraints

WHEN to apply this attack

This attack is a more general form of the previous attack. Instead of concentrating on overflowing size, we are concerned with investigating *all* the access points to *any* constraint on the data structure, including its size. Such constraints can be size, dimension, type, shape, location on the screen, and so forth. Indeed, we are interested in any property of a structure that a user can set and that should be constrained within a set of parameters. For example, an array should have between one and twelve elements, a "year" data value should fall within the range 1980 to 2095, or the limit of "undo" operations should be twenty.

> **Investigating alternative ways to modify internal data constraints** will test that error code is in place, not only when data is created but also when data is accessed or edited. Just because error code is correctly written for when a data structure is created does not mean that the developer included that code for when the data is modified. If the error code is not correct in all places in which the object can be edited, this attack will find those bugs.

Whenever any such constraints on stored data can be identified, this attack applies.

WHAT software faults make this attack successful?

Constraints on data properties are checked any time a data item is established and with any subsequent modification of the data item. Developers are usually very good about checking data items when they are created. However, too often they neglect to do so when the data item is modified.

The reason this happens is that creation of a data object and subsequent modification are done by different functions, or at least different sections of code within the same function. The code to check constraints must be included in both places. Although this seems trivial, it often is overlooked on projects in which several developers are working on the same object and not communicating about how they are programming constraints.

A more common scenario is that errors exist in initialization code and modification code, but when a bug is reported, the only fix made is to the initialization component, and the modification of other components is overlooked. This is a common theme whenever code is duplicated: A fix in one location isn't propagated to every occurrence of the code in question.

HOW to determine if this attack exposes failures

Broken data constraints are serious. The effect of invalid data on a system is often catastrophic, resulting in a system crash. However, testers should also look for delayed response time, incorrect error messages (that is, the software detects that something is wrong but has no idea what), and invalid output generated when the software tries to use the bad data in an internal computation.

HOW to conduct this attack

The first item of business for a tester is to identify candidate data and list their changeable properties. For each property, testers must ask certain questions. What are the allowable ranges of valid values? Under what constraints does the data operate? Are there certain contexts in which the data can exist?

The answers to these questions will give testers an idea of the constraints that govern the range of values that each property can legally assume. Next, document when the property is initially set and all the places in which the properties of that data can be changed. This can be time consuming, given only black box knowledge of behavior. One must infer when data is initialized and when it is being modified.

The next step is pretty obvious. Testers must use the application in ways that force the data to be initialized. Once initialized, each property should be changed to determine if the constraints are being enforced.

My colleague Alan Jorgensen likes the phrase "the right hand knoweth not what the left hand doeth" to describe this class of bugs. An excellent example is the crashing bug that one of my students found in PowerPoint regarding the size of tabular data. The act of creating the table is constrained to 25×25 as the maximum size. However, one can create such a table, then add rows and columns to it from another location in the program—crashing the application. The right hand knew better than to allow a 26×26 table, but the left hand wasn't aware of the rule.

Try this by firing up PowerPoint and inserting a 25×25 table (see Fig. 3.3).

FIGURE 3.3

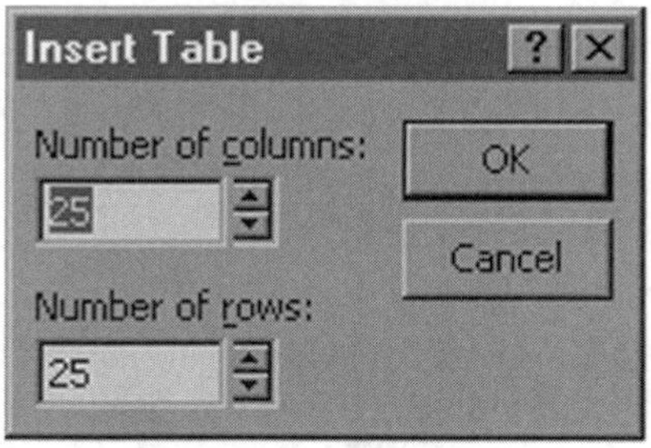

While you are at it, run the long-string attack and character-set attack against these dialogs. They cannot be broken, although you might notice some strange behaviors (for example, the default is either two or twenty-five, and the logic behind the choice isn't easy to decipher). Once you insert the table, notice the toolbox that appears, allowing you to edit the table (see Fig. 3.4).

FIGURE 3.4

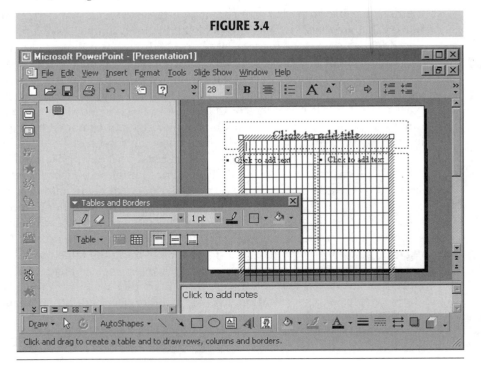

Inserting one row and one column is usually enough to lock up PowerPoint irretrievably (see Fig. 3.5).

FIGURE 3.5

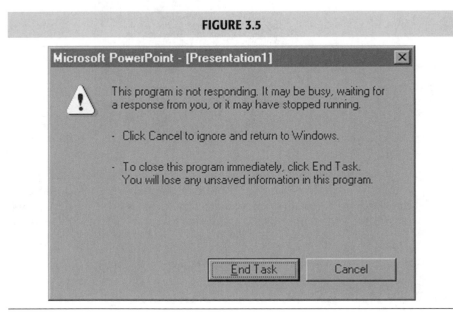

Exploring Computation and Feature Interaction

Computation, using operands stored internally and operands received as input from users, is one of the most fundamental tasks that software performs. It presents challenging testing problems. Like data, computation cannot be directly seen. It is hidden behind the user interface, and much of the details associated with a particular computation must be surmised without benefit of the source code.

Computation occurs everywhere in a software application. Computation is performed in assignment statements, which pervade all code no matter what the functionality. Software computes when it loops, when it branches, and when its features interact with its stored data. The next three attacks will put some perspective on the difficult endeavor of testing software computation.

ATTACK 14 Experiment with invalid operand and operator combinations

WHEN to apply this attack

This attack applies when you can identify computation (that is, operators) involving specific data or inputs (that is, operands). The idea is to experiment with operator/operand combinations that may cause the software to fail.

Identifying such computations doesn't always mean looking for mathematical expressions in source code, although math expressions are an obvious candidate for this attack. Indeed, math takes place is some unlikely places. Any type of graphical rendering is computation intensive, and there are many practical examples. Consider, for example, computing text placement in a word processor. One must consider things like page boundaries, margins, font size, and so forth as operands to whatever internal

> **Experimenting with invalid operand and operator combinations** will verify that internal computations do not take place with incorrect data values. Dividing by zero is a simple case of an operand (for example, zero) being incompatible with the operator (for example, division). Because all operators have an expected set of legal operands with which they can correctly function, testing the invalid cases will help ensure that none of these problems will surface after release.

computation places text on a page. Thus this attack is much more universally applicable than it first appears to be.

Computations that have more than one operand are even more vulnerable to this attack because there is the chance that the operands may conflict with each other. For example, character and number types can be combined with the "+" operator in many programming languages. In the former case, adding characters causes them to be concatenated. In the latter case, integer arithmetic is performed. However, forcing a software system to add a character to a number (that is, conflicting operands) might cause a failure.

WHAT software faults make this attack successful?

Given a specific operator, developers must write significant error-checking code when they use the operator on a given set of operands. The divide-by-zero error is the classic example. Division (that is, the operator) using any numeric operand other than zero works just fine. Developers must always remember to wrap all divisions in an "if" statement that precludes its operation with the operand zero. Failure to do so will crash the application.

Almost every operator has its invalid operands, and it only takes one developer who is unaware of them to have a bug in your application.

HOW to determine if this attack exposes failures

Performing an invalid operation usually causes a complete software crash. However, if a global exception handler keeps an application alive after this attack is successful, it likely means missing or incorrect data or an unintelligible error message.

HOW to conduct this attack

First, identify the places in which computation occurs and get a general idea of what data is used. The idea is to ensure that the data is varied in ways that will achieve your desired result: The operation will use invalid operand values.

To illustrate this attack, consider the calculator shipped with Windows. Let's concentrate on the square-root operator (inverse x^2). My hypothesis is that in conversion from integer operands to floating-point results, some precision will be lost. The square-root function is a convenient one to test because we also have a square function, which we can use as an oracle to verify that we are getting the right answer.

Taking the square root of two is a good test because the answer is a very long real number (see Fig 3.6).

FIGURE 3.6

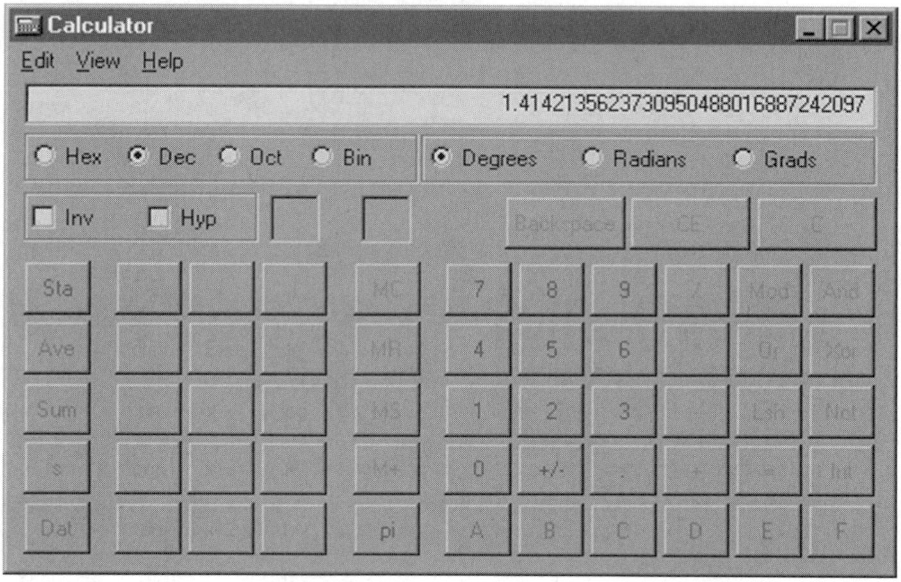

Squaring that result gives us the desired answer of two again. We square two once more, and we get another expected answer of four (see Fig. 3.7).

FIGURE 3.7

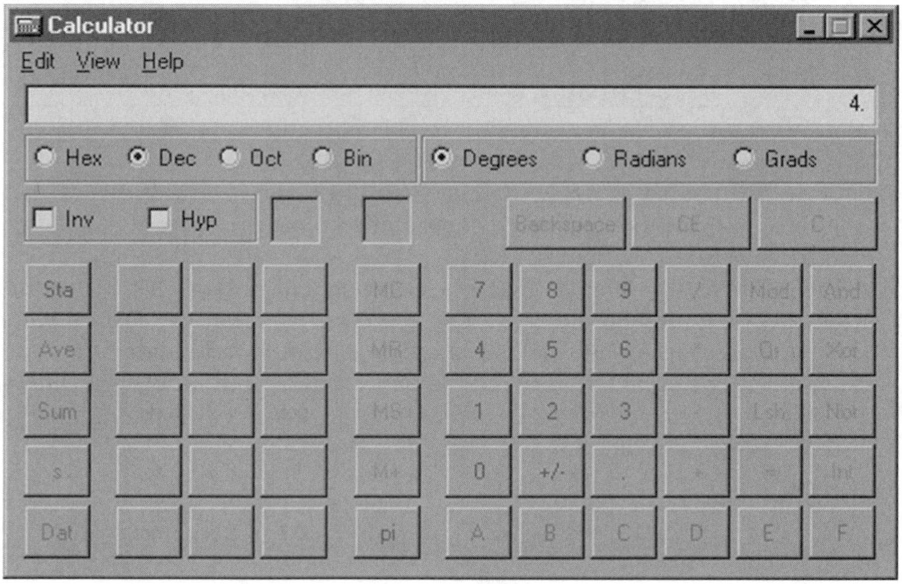

However, four is only the displayed answer. The actual value stored is different from four, which we can verify by pressing "minus four." We all know that four minus four equals zero. Because the answer is a number not equal to zero, we just verified our hypothesis that precision is being lost. To reproduce this, put the calculator in scientific mode and type, two, Inv (a check box in the upper left corner), x^2, x^2, x^2, minus sign, four, and the equal sign. See Fig. 3.8 for the result.

FIGURE 3.8

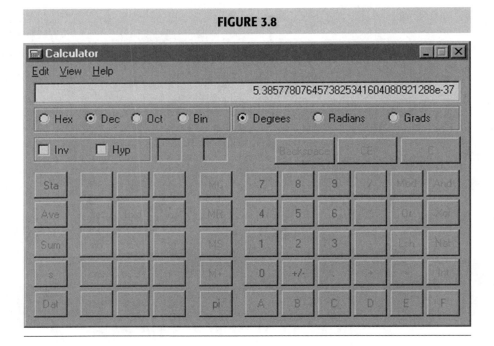

The answer is not zero. It is close, but it is not zero. If this calculation were part of a long series of computations, the rounding would likely get a lot worse.

The real problem is that when the calculator displayed the rounded number, it masked the error from the user. The user sees four, but the calculator has an internal variable that is storing a number that is not four. When stored values and displayed values get out of sync, the user is tricked into a false sense of security and may rely on the numbers as being accurate when they are not.

ATTACK 15   Force a function to call itself recursively

WHEN to apply this attack

Functions often call other functions to get work done. Sometimes functions call themselves. This is called recursion, and it is a powerful alternative for iterative loops that developers often employ. Loops and recursion can be problematic if the number of times they execute is not limited to a finite number. The "infinite loop" is a common programming error. However, such things are generally well covered in unit testing. As a system tester, it has been many years since I saw such a problem go unfixed long enough to get to me.

> **Forcing a function to call itself recursively** may expose serious design flaws. Even though an object can interact with other objects, it might be that an object cannot interact with itself or a copy of itself. If the developers failed to write code to handle that special case, the code may break when such recursion is tested.

Recursion, however, is another story. Modern software applications offer ways for objects to reference themselves, which in turn offer testers new ways to break them.

The hyperlink is the most common analogy. Imagine a Web page that has a link to itself. This is the general idea of recursion. Now imagine a Web page with a script that automatically executes when the page is displayed. Suppose that script reloads its host page . . . which executes the script . . . which reloads the host page . . . which executes the script . . . . You get the idea. This shows the danger of recursion. If it is implemented improperly, it will quickly overwhelm the resources of the machine and eventually generate a heap overflow.

WHAT software faults make this attack successful?

The major cause of this class of bugs is that developers fail to write code that guarantees that loops and recursive calls terminate. The term "infinite loop" describes this class of problem. The problem is usually a missing if-then-else block or other conditional check at the beginning or end of the loop that decides if the computation is finished.

HOW to determine if this attack exposes failures

This bug manifests itself as a heap overflow in the computer's memory. A heap overflow causes the application to crash or hang, and it will have to be forcibly terminated.

HOW to conduct this attack

Like many computation attacks, domain knowledge and experience is crucial, so begin by learning the problem domain as well as you can. Often recursion is hidden in the most advanced application features.

The first step is to make a list of features that you think may have embedded recursion. Because recursion is an action, think about action words such as "reference" (that is, an object can reference another object). An object can "contain" another object. An object can "point to" another object. An object can "spawn," "process," "link," "possess," and so forth.

Once identified, it is your task to force referencing, spawning, and so forth that never ends. The simplest way is for an object to reference itself. Can a spreadsheet cell contain a formula that uses that cell position in the formula? Can a word processing document contain a reference to itself?

Consider the following C program fragment:

```
long int factorial(int n)
{
    if (n <= 1)
        return(1);
    else
        return(n * factorial(n - 1));
}
```

Notice that the recursive `return(n * factorial(n - 1))` is executed within the "else" block of the code. This ensures that the recursion only occurs after the check has been made to see if the computation is complete. Thus this program is correct. Take out the "if" statement, and it will cause an infinite loop.

As an example, insert a footnote within a footnote in Microsoft Word. One might presume that this behavior would be prevented. However, it is allowed, and the behavior is quite strange (see Figs. 3.9 and 3.10).

Note that inserting a footnote within a footnote causes the note to get a new number, but no new footnote is generated.

FIGURE 3.9

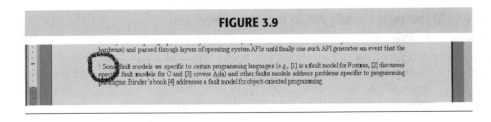

FIGURE 3.10

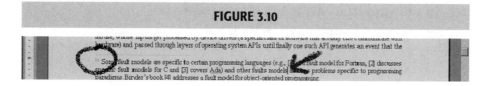

ATTACK 16   Force computation results to be too large or too small

WHEN to apply this attack

The next computation attack is aimed at overflowing and underflowing data objects that store computation results. The target this time is not the operators or operands but the *result* of the computation.

Consider a simple equation:

```
sum = sum + value[i]
```

> **Forcing computation results to be too large or too small** will often overflow the storage set aside for the result of the computation. Even a simple statement like $x=x+1$ will overflow the value of x if the computation is performed enough.

Suppose that `value[i]` is an array of values supplied as input to the program and that `sum` is an internally stored result.

The input attacks we applied earlier will ensure that we test for boundary and illegal values of `value[i]`. Likewise, applying the data attacks will thoroughly test `sum`. However, this code can still be made to fail. This is really the crux of this attack: Input and data can be correctly constrained, and computation can still fail.

This attack is applicable in those very cases where an application performs computations that cause a result to be produced and stored internally.

WHAT software faults make this attack successful?

 How can software fail when all data and input are valid? The answer lies in the *result* of the computation. Even though all data used in the computation are valid, data can still be combined in ways to cause the result to be invalid.

Consider the simplest of equations: $x=x+1$. If you execute this line of code enough, eventually the memory set aside for the result x will overflow the maximum value allowed for that variable. All variables have an upper limit, and sometimes developers forget to check this limit when performing computations. They may remember it when validating the input or validating stored data, but validating the result of a computation can be more difficult.

The same thing applies to the negative end of a data type. The equation $y=x-1$ will fail if we assign x the value $-32,768$.

HOW to determine if this attack exposes failures

Because this attack forces overflow or underflow, the software will often crash when you are successful. You'll also find that developers seldom write exception handlers around computations because they cannot fathom how the equation could fail when the input and data are correct. The lack of error-handling code makes a crash very likely.

HOW to conduct this attack

This attack usually requires you to force a computation to occur over and over or force it to occur using very large or very small inputs and data. Begin at or around boundary values of data types to speed up the search.

Consider the program:

```
const count 2
main() {
    int sum, value[count];
    sum = 0;
    for (i = 0; i < count; ++i) {
        sum = sum + value[i];
    }
}
```

Either of the following data sets will cause this program to crash.

```
value[0] = 32700, value[1] = 70
count = 33000, value[0..32999] = 1
```

The former will cause the result of 32,770, which is larger that 32,767. The latter will cause the result to also grow out of bounds—albeit using much more data—until the result is 33,000.

ATTACK **17**   Find features that share data or interact poorly

WHEN to apply this attack

A feature can be tested in isolation—without considering how other features might affect its behavior—using any or all of the attacks discussed. However, the feature could well be buggy when it is used in combination with other features in the same software.

> **Testing feature interaction** means finding inputs that cause one feature to share data or resources with another feature that causes at least one of the features to break. The idea is to identify common characteristics of features and test to see that the features cannot break each other when these common characteristics are forced to interact.

This attack is applicable whenever an application can do more than one thing at the same time or when more than one feature can be active at the same time. For example, a word processor can produce a document with footnotes (one feature) and dual columns (another feature) on the same page. Although these two features may work fine by themselves, their interaction with each another may fail.

WHAT software faults make this attack successful?

Feature interaction failures are most often caused when two or more features work with a shared set of data and each feature enforces a different set of constraints on that data. For example, one feature may constrain a data item to a specific size, whereas a second feature may allow the size to grow beyond the ability of the first feature to handle it. What really happens is that developers are unaware that the data can be modified elsewhere. Thus they write code to ensure that their feature never breaks the constraints on the data, but they fail to check those constraints when they use the data. This is fine when only their feature is active, but when another feature modifies the shared data, all bets are off.

The fix for developers is easy enough. All constraint checking must be done when the data is modified and when the data is used. That way no matter what feature changes the data, invalid data will never be used. Unfortunately, thinking through all the possible feature-to-data interactions is an enormous task, and often some relationships are overlooked.

HOW to determine if this attack exposes failures

As with many of the prior attacks, testers are again stuck with painstaking screen verification when conducting this attack. Moreover, failures due to feature interaction can be subtle, and the point at which the fault manifests itself as a failure can often be delayed over many subsequent inputs. Testers must keep a sharp eye out for bad output formatting, incorrect computations, and corrupted data.

HOW to conduct this attack

The ability to conduct this attack often separates testing novices from the pros. The problem is nothing new: Different application features share the same data space, and through differing assumptions about the disposition of the data or through the generation of undesirable side effects, the inter-action of the two features causes the application to fail.

However, which features share data and interpret it in conflicting ways is an open question in testing. The following general guidelines are helpful:

1. Ask if the same inputs can be applied to each feature in question. If the features have overlapping input domains, they may well have prob-lems interacting.

2. Ask if there are similar outputs that can be produced using each of the features in question. If there are features that combine to produce a single output, the features are related and should be tested together.

3. Ask if a feature can get in the way of another feature's computation. The "get in the way" metaphor is a handy way of thinking about fea-ture interaction with respect to computation. For example, if you are testing an application's ability to use the mouse to select text on the screen, you might want to put other objects "in the way" of the cursor as it is dragged across a section of text. Putting hyperlinked text, for-matted text (for example, bold, italics, symbols), or graphical objects in the path of the cursor may be a fruitful test.

The general idea is to use one feature to affect the input, output, data, or computation of another feature.

Fig. 3.11 shows an unexpected result when combining footnotes and dual columns on a single page in Word 2000. The problem is that Word

FIGURE 3.11

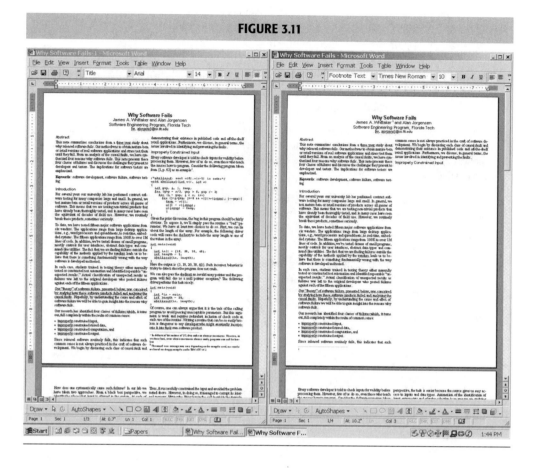

computes the page width of a footnote from the reference point of the note. Thus if there are two footnotes on the same page, one referenced from a dual-column location and one referenced from a single-column location, the single-column footnote pushes the dual-column footnote to the next page. Also pushed to the next page is any text between the note's reference point and the bottom of the page.

Fig. 3.11 illustrates the problem vividly. Where is the second column of text? It is on the next page along with the footnote. Can you live with the document looking like this? You'll have to unless you find a workaround, which means time spent away from preparing your document.

Other examples in Word 2000 include problems with widow or orphan control on paragraphs with embedded pictures and resizing text boxes that have been grouped with other types of objects.

Summary of the Data/Computation Attacks—A Checklist for Battle

Data Attacks

11. Pick an input. Think about all the situations in which the input can be applied. Test the software by applying the input under as many of these conditions as possible. Think of situations in which the input should not be applicable. Apply it anyway.

12. "Look through" the interface and identify data structures, or review the source code if it is available. For any given data structure, store too many or too few values in it. Applying too many values means that you must identify a preset limit. Storing too few values means adding data and deleting it all, then deleting again.

13. Determine constraints on data-structure creation and usage. Find other ways (using other parts of the software or even other applications) to modify the data so that you violate these constraints.

Computation Attacks

14. Find a place where computation is occurring and force an operator to be paired with conflicting operands or multiple operands that cannot coexist for a given operator.

15. Force an internal function to call itself recursively. Include a document within itself, make a hyperlink point to itself, and so forth.

16. Force a computation to occur that overflows the storage available to receive the result of the computation.

17. Pick a feature and think of other features that get in its way.

■■ Conclusion

The data and computation attacks presented in this chapter present serious challenges to software testers. Testers must "look through" the user interface and imagine what data and computation is taking place. Testers who master this technique will be able to find serious bugs in their software.

Data and computation-oriented bugs are serious because they greatly influence the software's ability to perform its prescribed tasks. Bugs that cause software to corrupt data or incorrectly compute a result are bugs that need to be kicked back to development for further analysis.

■■ Exercises

Professional testers can use whatever software application they are working on to perform these exercises. Students can choose any application they use frequently. At Florida Tech, we choose an application in advance for our semester-long class, and everyone in the class works on it, usually in teams of two.

Once you have selected your application under test, perform the following exercises. Just for fun, we'll refer to the application under test as the "target."

1. *These exercises are a continuation of the exercises in Chapter 2.* Pretend you are a user and use your target application. Think like a real user and use the application to get real work done. While you are doing this, make a note of the inputs that you are applying. A good way to organize the inputs is by feature. Make a table of features and list the inputs that can be applied to each one. For example, if you are testing the "Find/Replace" feature of a word processor, your inputs would be <find string>, <replace string>, <ok button>, <cancel button>, and so forth.

2. Use the table you created in Exercise 1 above and add a new column to it to document data structures that each feature uses. Look through the input and output attacks you ran and see how many data structures you tested during those attacks.

3. Apply each of the data attacks to your application. Document the attacks that you applied, the features that worked as specified, and the bugs you found.

4. Continue using your table from the previous exercises and add a new column to it to document computations that each feature uses. Look through the input, output, and data attacks you ran and see how much computation you forced during those attacks.

5. Apply each of the computation attacks to your application. Document the attacks that you applied, the features that worked as specified, and the bugs you found.

6. Pick a programming language like C++, Java, or Visual Basic. Make a list of the operators that the language supports. For each operator, list the ranges for valid and invalid operands. For which attack would you use such a list?

PART 3

System Interface Attacks

CHAPTER 4
Testing from the File System Interface

0110010111011100010100

Attacking Software from the File System Interface

Most testers are much more comfortable with the attacks from the user interface we covered in Chapters 2 and 3 than with the attacks we are about to embark on. Indeed, many testers ignore attacks from the file system interface, assuming that files will not be a source of problems for their application. But files and the file system can cause an application to fail. The inputs from a file or file system are in every way, shape, and form the same as inputs from the human user. File system and user interfaces share the common trait that if the input they supply is out of the expected range, the software can fail.

Failure associated with file system inputs can be particularly troublesome. Files are the only way that users can permanently store their data. Mishandling of files by software can result in data corruption, which is probably the most serious type of software failure.

Testing file interaction is therefore an important endeavor when data integrity and data loss are issues for the end user. This chapter discusses attacks that test software's ability to carry out the important work of reading and writing files.

File system attacks are divided into two categories: *media-based attacks* and *file-based attacks,* both of which are described in detail below.

Media-based Attacks

Media-based attacks aim to simulate problems with the storage media itself—the floppy disk, hard disk, CD-ROM, and so forth. Media failures can occur as a result of faulty software drivers or actual physical damage to the media caused by scratches, dirt, overuse, or lack of proper maintenance, for example.

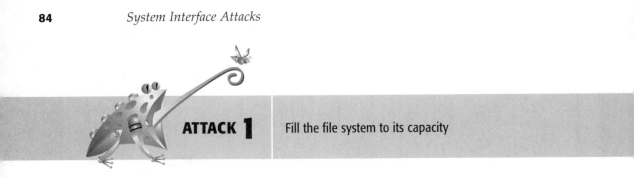

ATTACK **1**   Fill the file system to its capacity

WHEN to apply this attack

Hard drives seem enormous these days. Tens and even hundreds of giga-bytes are the norm, terabytes are on the short-term horizon, and there is no reason to believe that this trend won't continue. It seems strange to discuss such a file system at full capacity, but filling a huge drive is much more common than one might think.

> **Filling the file system to its capacity** will ensure your application gracefully handles a full disk. Once a full disk is simulated by Canned HEAT, you should try to force the application to open, close, read, write, and modify at every opportunity. This way you can find places where files are accessed but the software fails to check for a full disk.

A file system can get full over time. You'd be surprised how many users never empty their recycle bin and operate with a severely fragmented hard disk. Yet if users see your software misbehaving as the first symptom of such a problem, they will place the blame squarely on your application.

The files users save are also getting bigger. For example, users routine-ly archive entire web sites in order to save the content before the sites get updated. The bigger our hard drives grow, the more voracious our appetite for storage becomes.

Moreover, many applications, such as embedded software, real-time software, and applications for handheld devices, do not enjoy an over-abundance of storage. Indeed, handheld applications often work with only the barest amounts of memory. An application's ability to detect and react to limited or nonexistent disk space is therefore important.

To avoid these problems, many good developers write code that is capable of detecting and reacting to a stressed file system. Often this code goes untested because testers are unaware of the need for such testing or they have no convenient mechanism for causing overloaded file system failures. This attack is designed to give testers insight into testing an application when the file system is at capacity.

WHAT software faults make this attack successful?

Most developers have better machines than their users and are accustomed to an overabundance of storage. They may forget to write code to handle a full file system because it doesn't enter their minds that this situation could ever actually occur. Thus, they completely omit such error checking code on operating system APIs such as CreateFile, WriteFile, and so forth. Without that code, when a full file system does manifest itself, API calls fail and the software crashes without warning.

Also, because these extreme error cases are hard to test, they often go untested in unit testing. Thus, the error handling code itself may contain more mundane bugs that need to be found by testers.

HOW to determine if this attack exposes failures

Because much of the error code associated with a full file system goes untested, even the most common and simple bugs can propagate to released code. Thus, testers should be ready for anything when applying this attack.

One thing is for sure: Operating systems *will* raise an error for an over-full file system. The question is whether our application will handle that error or go belly-up. Testers must be vigilant when running test cases with a near capacity storage medium. Anything can happen.

HOW to conduct this attack

The first step in conducting this or any file system attack is to understand all the situations under which your application accesses the file system for input or output. Some situations are clearly presented as file operations: Menu items such as "Open . . . ," "Save," "Save As . . . ," and "New" fall into this category. Harder to identify are file reads and writes that the application launches automatically. Operations such as an auto-save feature (which might automatically write user data every five minutes), callout labels (which operate when the mouse hovers over a screen object), or simple page-swapping (see the Glossary) all cause files to be accessed without user input. To find these file calls, testers can watch for the drive light on the computer to illuminate, look through source code, or ask developers about when these operations occur within the application.

The obvious way to perform this attack is to create a file system at or near capacity and then force it to access files. Although file writes are the obvious choice to fill the system, because they will increase the size of the files stored on disk, file opens can sometimes force backup copies to be created, doubling the storage used. When enough such increases have occurred, you will reach the system's capacity and will be able to test the application's ability to handle the situation of a full file system.

Maintaining the large files necessary to perform this testing can be cumbersome, however. If the files are kept on the system, then you'll have a computer that is unusable for anything but testing this scenario—hardly worth the loss of a computer. If you delete the files and regenerate them each time, you incur the cost of this work each time you want to test this scenario.

For those reasons, simulation is a sound choice for many of the file system attacks. We will discuss simulation by using the tool Canned HEAT, included on the CD-ROM that accompanies this book. Before using Canned HEAT, read Appendixes A and B to familiarize yourself with the concept and use of runtime fault injection.

The following example (shown in Figures 4.1 through 4.6) demonstrates Canned HEAT's ability to dish out fault injected attacks and the ability of Microsoft Internet Explorer to handle them.

FIGURE 4.1

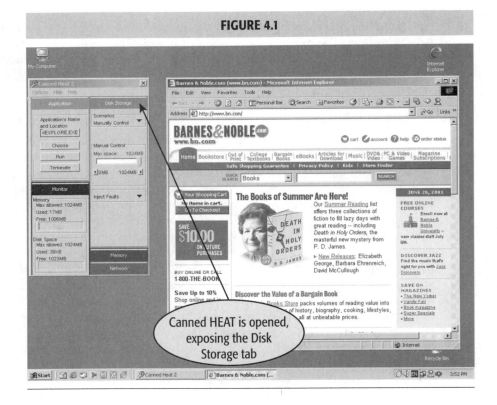

FIGURE 4.2

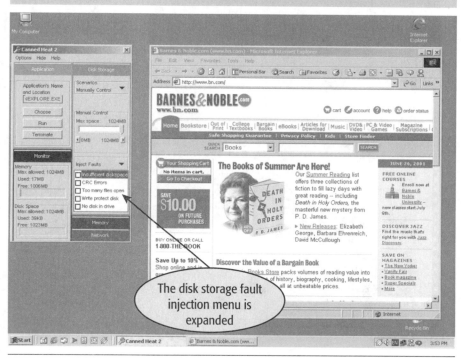

The disk storage fault injection menu is expanded

FIGURE 4.3

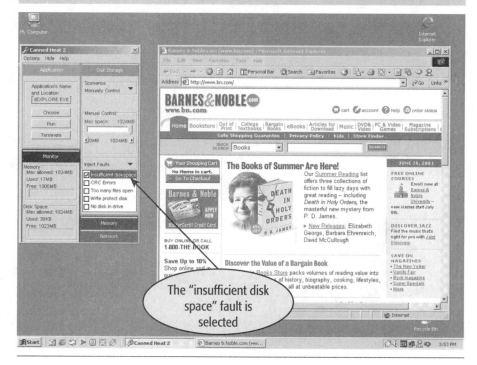

The "insufficient disk space" fault is selected

FIGURE 4.4

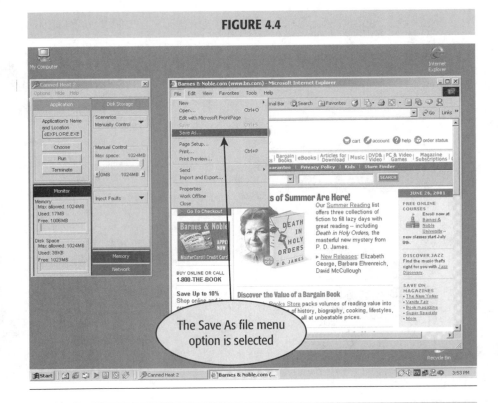

The Save As file menu option is selected

FIGURE 4.5

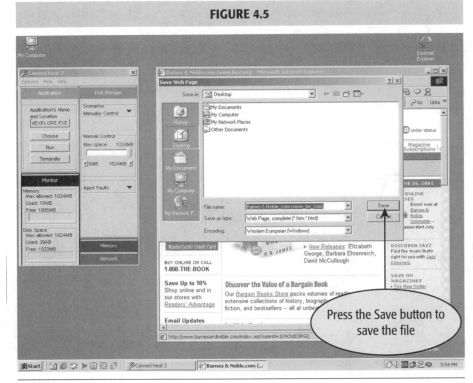

Press the Save button to save the file

FIGURE 4.6

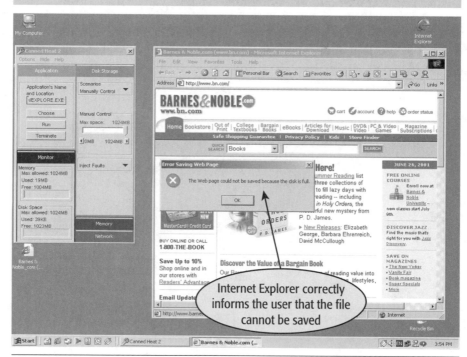

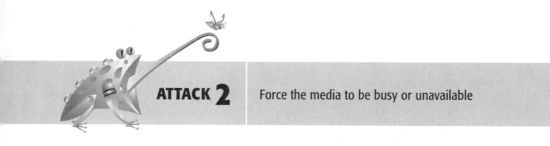

ATTACK 2   Force the media to be busy or unavailable

WHEN to apply this attack

Modern operating systems can run many applications simultaneously (this is called multitasking). Some applications run in the background and are invisible to the user. These applications are usually called *services*. User

> **Forcing the media to be busy or unavailable** will ensure that error conditions related to a problematic storage device get tested. The idea is to force error return codes indicating problems with the media when the application accesses a hard drive, floppy drive, or other external storage mechanism. If developers fail to write proper error handling routines for these conditions, the application will fail.

applications can also run simultaneously, and the user can swap them from the background to the foreground (so they can be used) using whatever operating system convention they prefer.

In Windows, Alt-Tab can be used to switch between foreground and background applications that the user has launched. In addition, the Task Manager can be used to view all the applications that are running on the system at any given time. The Task Manager appears in Fig. 4.7 and is viewed on Windows NT/2000/XP by pressing Ctrl-Shift-Esc.

FIGURE 4.7

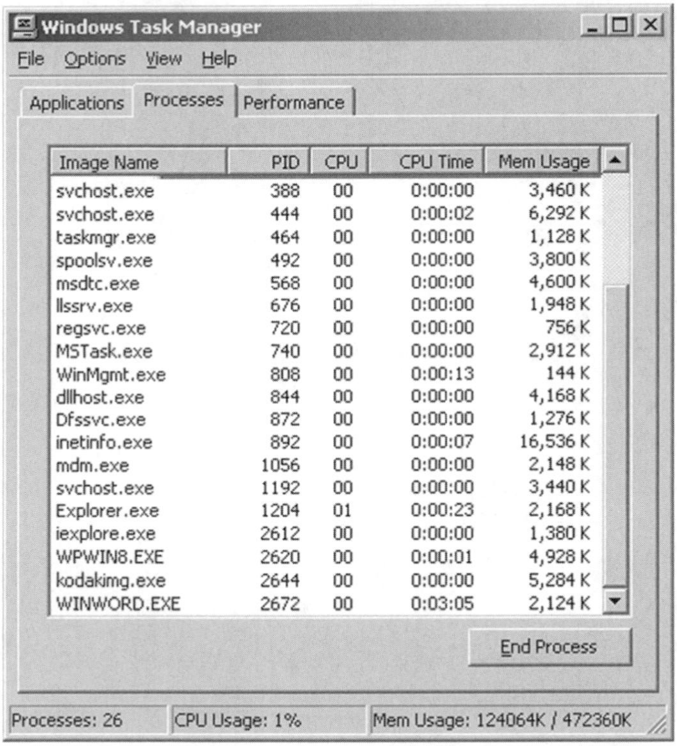

The fact that all these applications and background services are running at the same time as your application can cause problems. Of course, it would be nice if all users concentrated only on your application, but that's not realistic. We need to be able to test for interoperability issues that arise from modern multitasking operating systems.

WHAT software faults make this attack successful?

From the perspective of the file system, the problem is that multiple applications are accessing the hard drive (or other storage) simultaneously. The operating system will be slow to service the multiple requests, and applications must be programmed to deal with these delays. When the delays become excessive, errors are generated. Applications that are not programmed to respond to these errors will fail.

HOW to determine if this attack exposes failures

Testing for such interoperability problems requires us to create contention for file system resources so that delayed response times will result. Small delays should be anticipated and not interpreted by testers as bugs. Uncommonly large delays, however, without some error message or wait indicator, are bugs and need to be reported.

When errors (instead of just delays) are returned by the operating system, expect your application to generate an error message or watch to see if it fails.

HOW to conduct this attack

Again we have the choice between actually creating the failing scenario or simulating it with Canned HEAT. Again we find that, with the same tradeoffs, simulation is a faster and easier way to accomplish this attack.

File system contention can be created by launching a number of applications along with a few copies of your own application and forcing them all to open and save files. You can vary the location of the files and also generate background traffic by starting a big download. (I like to use *www.download.com*; they have lots of downloads that take several minutes or more.)

Of course, you can also use Canned HEAT. One of the faults that Canned HEAT is able to inject is "too many files open." This fault is one of a number of memory faults (covered in the next chapter) and file system faults that can arise because of application contention for resources. Each file system has a maximum number of files that it can have open at any one time; once this number is exceeded, the operating system will return an error message. As you can see next, an application's inability to handle this error message can have noteworthy consequences.

FIGURE 4.8

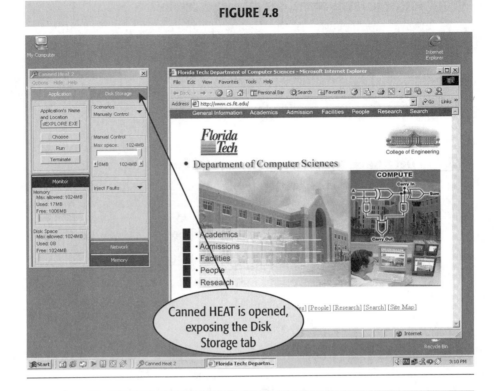

Canned HEAT is opened, exposing the Disk Storage tab

FIGURE 4.9

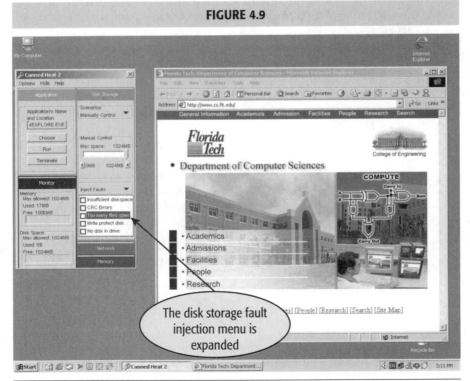

The disk storage fault injection menu is expanded

FIGURE 4.10

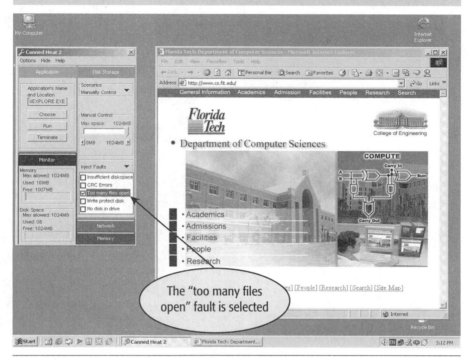

The "too many files open" fault is selected

FIGURE 4.11

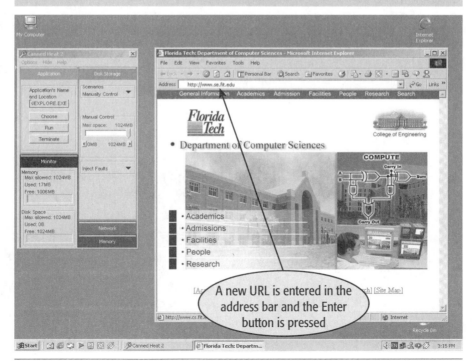

A new URL is entered in the address bar and the Enter button is pressed

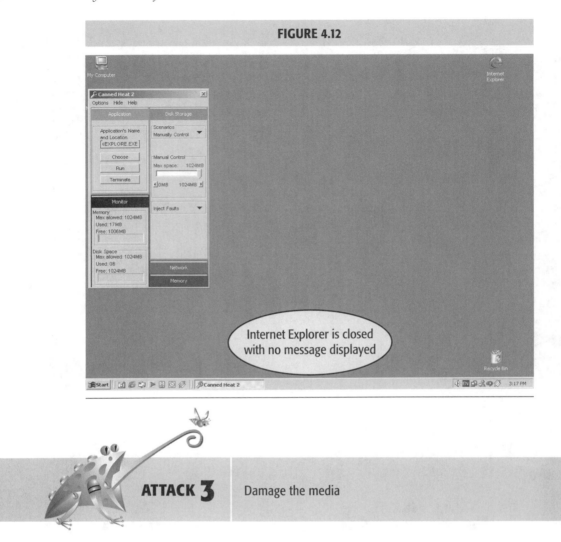

FIGURE 4.12

Internet Explorer is closed
with no message displayed

ATTACK **3**   Damage the media

WHEN to apply this attack

This attack sounds ominous, and it is probably not one many companies
will require you to deploy. Indeed, going to such extremes is something I
have seen only certain vendors do: creators of operating systems, device

> **Simulating damaged storage media** is useful for mission-critical
> applications where the software must still work despite damaged
> media. This attack will help to test for cases in which the developers
> failed to write error handling code when files are accessed or written.

drivers/controllers, and safety-critical applications being among the folks who apply such an attack.

The main consideration in determining whether to apply this attack is the importance of data to your users. If you are supplying data (and storing it on a permanent storage medium like a hard drive) that is mission-critical and whose loss could cause irreparable harm to your customers (and therefore to you), you need to consider this attack.

WHAT software faults make this attack successful?

This attack is one of the few that not only can be successful because of bugs in your software, but also can be successful even if your software is perfect (which it could never be; see Appendix C). On the one hand, a damaged medium may cause the operating system to pass back an error code that your application is not programmed to handle, a typical failure of omitting the error handling code discussed in the previous two attacks. On the other hand, the operating system may not be able to detect all such errors reliably. Indeed, the operating system itself may have bugs that prevent it from detecting damaged media. Worse, the damaged medium may actually corrupt part of the operating system.

Moreover, even if the software and operating system can handle all the errors that might be generated by damaged media, data can still be corrupted beyond recovery. Even though your application is not responsible for the damaged disk, it will get blamed for losing data.

HOW to determine if this attack exposes failures

As with the previous two attacks, when an error is generated, the application will either handle it and inform the user of the problem, or it will crash. This attack has the additional requirement that we must check user data files to determine if any data is lost or corrupted.

HOW to conduct this attack

Canned HEAT does not simulate this attack. Thus, should you choose to implement this attack (and most testers do not), you must actually create the attack situation. Namely, identify the ways to get the software to access files and then force it to do so with damaged media. Common disk-oriented problems are dust, dirt, scratches, and magnetic scrambling. Get out your magnets and dust bunnies and go at it.

File-based Attacks

Almost any nontrivial software system uses files. Some files are very visible because they store user data. The user explicitly names those files and uses the names to locate the files the next time that data is needed. These user files normally have a recognizable file extension such as .xls or .doc. There are other files the user does not see at all. An application often uses files under-the-covers to store user preferences, backup data, and so forth. Testers cannot afford to be unaware of these "invisible" files because they could be the source of faults that keep our software from properly delivering its functionality.

Some research on your application is in order to determine what the "invisible" files are named and where they are stored. As a rule of thumb, temporary backup files are usually stored in the same directory as the user files. Customization and preference files are stored in folders determined by the application. There are template folders and preference folders, among others, that can be stored in general system folders or in a user's account folder.

Once you've identified these files, apply these attacks to each file.

ATTACK 4   Assign an invalid file name

WHEN to apply this attack

Whether your application provides a mechanism for the user to enter a file name or the user performs this operation directly through the OS, file names are variable input and invalid names must be considered by your application. If your application tries to process a file name that it is not equipped to handle, trouble will ensue.

File names are processed whenever an application opens, reads, writes, or saves a file. If your application has any of these capabilities, then testing its ability to handle a diverse set of file names is a must.

> **Assigning an invalid file name** serves to find places in which there are no constraints on reading or writing files identifiers. Since file names are often restricted by the operating system, the failure to create valid names will cause failures if they are not constrained properly by an application. The idea is to try overly long names and names that include illegal characters and character combinations.

WHAT software faults make this attack successful?

The operating system itself carefully enforces naming conventions for files. Older operating systems restrict file names (for example, eight characters and a three-character extension). Windows and Unix have no such restrictions but nevertheless enforce certain rules about character combinations and length. Most file name related bugs result in cases where the developer used a different set of rules to govern file names than is used by the operating system. If the rules are too far out of sync, the application will try to write a file with an invalid name. When this occurs, the operating system will return an error to the application. If the application is not programmed to handle this error, it will crash.

HOW to determine if this attack exposes failures

This attack is made up of a single, very specific event: Assign an invalid file name and then try using (opening, writing, reading, or saving) the file. You will know immediately whether you get an error message. If you do not get an error message, the application will most often crash. You should also carefully check the files that are written to ensure they received the correct name, extension, and application associations.

HOW to conduct this attack

The first set of tests are to get the application to an equivalent of the "Save As . . ." dialog and enter names that are not acceptable to the operating system. Rerun the test for every such dialog, in case the developers are not using common code for the save function.

The second set of tests to run is to use the operating system to create (by renaming) files with valid file names that might not be acceptable by the application. This attack has much in common with the character set attack (attack 3), the long string attack (attack 4) and the input combination attack (attack 5) from Chapter 2.

As an example, consider the following odd behavior of almost all Windows applications I could find (demonstrated using Word for continuity). In Windows, file names can have many different characters: alphanumeric characters, spaces, and so on. Further, Windows uses the file extension to identify which application can open a file. So, for example, Word automatically gives the extension ".doc" to any file saved in Word. Some combinations of characters, however, can make Word (and any other Windows application) goof up. The magic in the example is the combination of semicolon and dot characters. Both of these characters are perfectly legal individually; it is their combination that causes the application to incorrectly assign a file extension.

Here's the setup for Word: Open a new file and type any text you want. Next, choose the "Save As…" option from the file menu and type the file name `startrek;starwars-8.1.2001`, which in my example indicates that this document contains data taken on 8/1/2001 pertaining to two different science fiction subjects (I used dots to separate the date because the forward slash is not a legal character for file names). Because of the problematic combination of characters in its name, however, once the file is saved, it gets a generic Windows file extension and not the expected ".doc" extension. The main manifestation of this problem is that Word will be unable to detect the file as a Word file when the document is requested (see Fig. 4.13a), so users must know to display all files, not just Word files, when opening a document (see Fig. 4.13b).

FIGURE 4.13a

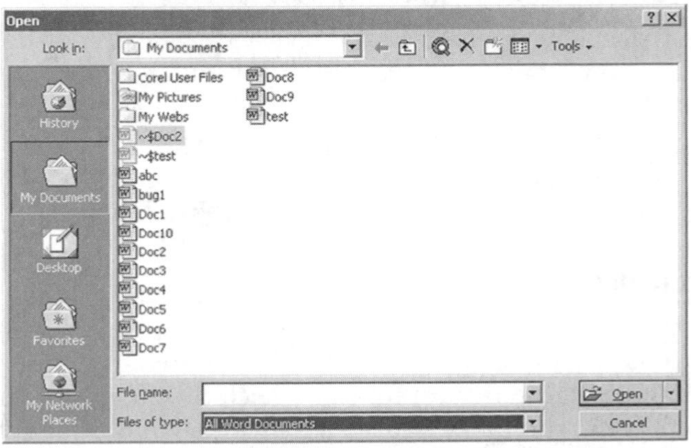

FIGURE 4.13b

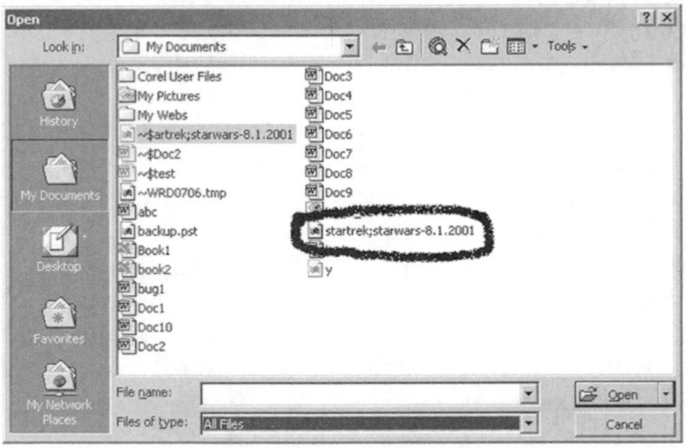

Note that the icon displayed in Fig. 4.13b does not associate our file with Word despite the fact that it was saved with Word in its native format.

ATTACK 5   Vary file access permissions

WHEN to apply this attack

Just as the file name (discussed in attack 4) is a property of a file, so are the permissions for a file. In modern operating systems, permissions can be set so that a particular user, user group, or administrative user is the only one who can access a file. Access rules can apply as well—for example, a file can be read-only or readable and writeable.

This attack applies to an application that has file access and whose files are accessible by multiple components within the application, by other applications, or by users directly through the operating system itself (in other words, by users accessing the file without going through the application under test).

WHAT software faults make this attack successful?

Multiple access/change points for file permissions open the door for programmer error. One component might open a file as read-only and another component might try to write data to it. Obviously, this will cause a problem unless the programmer thinks to check the permissions and access privileges of a file before each file write. If such checks are not made, failure may result.

HOW to determine if this attack exposes failures

If you apply this attack and see error messages pertaining to file permissions or trouble reading or writing a file, then the application has it right. Otherwise, you may see odd error messages characteristic of global exception handlers. Remember what we discussed about the problems with exception handlers (see attack 1 of Chapter 2, *Force all the error messages to occur*, to refresh your memory).

> **Varying file access permissions** will find subtle bugs that manifest when a file used by an application can be manipulated outside the control of that application. This attack focuses on establishing and changing file access permissions and then driving the application to access the file contents. If the error code to check for handling various permissions is missing or incorrect, the application will fail.

Of course, this attack often results in crashes. But few testers need to be reminded to look for these!

HOW to conduct this attack

The best bugs to find are bugs in which different components of the same application use different rules about file permissions. Unfortunately, this means going through each file that your application uses and forcing reads and writes from each feature of the application that hits the file. Painstaking to say the least, but bugs found using this technique will be important.

The second legitimate way to run this attack is to get two applications to break each other when they open the same file. The most common real-world version of this scenario is when different versions of the same application, installed together on the same machine, clash over file access permissions. Don't scoff at this scenario; some users keep multiple versions of their applications around to maintain backward compatibility. Testing whether old versions of your application break your current version can be a good way to find out what problems a user might experience when they keep multiple versions.

Testers can run this attack by opening and closing the same file in different applications and trying to open a file in one application while it is open in another.

Finally, it may be possible to change the file permissions through the operating system while a file is open. Some operating systems will permit a privileged user to take control of a file that a normal user has open. Thus, changing the permissions through the operating system is something you may want to try, but the chances of this occurring in the real world may be low.

ATTACK 6   Vary or corrupt file contents

WHEN to apply this attack

Software applications read and write files in the normal course of getting their work done. Applications read files at start-up to establish initial settings, configure the disposition of the GUI, and so forth. Conversely, applications also write files at termination in order to save any data for the next time the application starts up.

Files are also read and written intermittently during application use. Sometimes, the user directs such behavior by requesting a file to be opened or saved. At other times, the application initiates file activity on its own. For example, data may be stored in temporary files or read from pre-existing templates.

> **Varying and corrupting file contents** simulates files being modified intentionally (perhaps maliciously) or incidentally (for example, during transmission). If no error code has been written to check the file contents before they are read, then the software is likely to crash. Canned HEAT can be used to simulate these events so that the tester can force file operations and watch for possible failures.

WHAT software faults make this attack successful?

Developers write code to read from and write to files. They also write code that calls system APIs to obtain file pointers and open or close files. Any of these system APIs can fail or pass unexpected return values for any number of reasons. If developers fail to write code that verifies expected return values are passed back, then the application may fail due to an unhandled exception.

Unexpected return values might exist because a file is locked by another user, is write protected, or has access permissions that are too restrictive. File APIs can also fail for other, less mundane reasons, like the file is sitting on a bad sector of the hard drive or has improperly formatted data.

In addition to checking API return codes, developers must also write code to validate file format and contents. Formatting concerns include text versus binary, proper delimiters, and field values of the correct data type. Content issues deal mostly with whether the data being read is in the appropriate legal range for its intended purpose. For example, a numeric text file whose data is supposed to be positive real numbers should be validated so that any negative numbers in the file won't actually get processed.

If any of this code is incorrect or missing, the software may fail.

HOW to determine if this attack exposes failures

Failure to check return codes or to validate file format or contents often—but not always—crashes an application. Crashes are easy to detect; verifying other outcomes is more demanding.

Failure to validate an API return means that the application simply continues processing without the benefit of whatever work that API was supposed to perform. Thus, testers should look for data values that are corrupt (symbols displayed on the screen instead of strings or numbers) or even missing.

Failure to validate file format or content means that illegal data can get processed by the software under test. Misplaced delimiters will cause fields to be read in the wrong order and will often corrupt any internal computation that uses those values. Testers must look for incorrect answers being produced. Values out of range will cause similar problems.

Unfortunately, in the absence of a system crash, painstaking manual verification is often the only method to determine a failure.

HOW to conduct this attack

There are two basic ways to perform this attack—manually corrupt files or use runtime fault injection as files are being manipulated.

Manually corrupting files is almost always a static process. Start with a good file that the application has created and edit it. If the file is text, then a standard editor will do. Be sure to use an editor that is capable of interpreting the underlying character set (ASCII or UNICODE, for example). If the file is binary then a hex editor can be used.[1]

In either case, you'll want to modify both delimiters (spaces, commas, and semicolons are all commonly used delimiters) and actual field values. Delimiters can be removed, duplicated, added, and changed (which really means removing them). Field values should be treated just like they are treated when entered through the user interface. This means paying special attention to boundary values, special characters, and long strings.

Consider the crash scenario for Microsoft Excel® as shown in Fig. 4.14. The file that is open is corrupt. The bad block of data corresponds to the

FIGURE 4.14

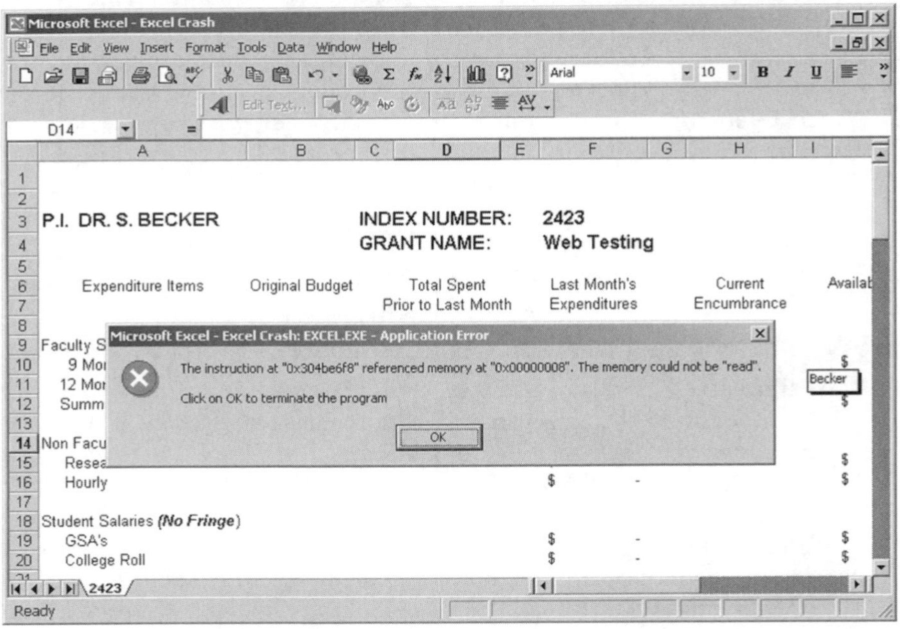

---

[1] You do not have to be that well versed in the hexadecimal encoding system to edit a binary file. Most hex editors come with a search and replace feature that converts your keystrokes to hex for you. You can thus simply search for a string and replace it with whatever you want, as easily as you could search and replace straight text.

label on the callout field labeled "Becker." When the mouse hovers over the label, Excel reads from a previously opened data file to retrieve the string to be displayed. However, the file system returns a CRC (cyclical redundancy check) error. Excel was obviously not programmed to handle such an event and crashes.

Canned HEAT can also be used to force invalid return codes for file APIs or to simulate CRC errors being thrown. Many formatting and content problems with files result in CRCs. Thus, runtime fault injection is a simple and accurate way to test for proper handling of corrupt files.

Summary of File System Attacks—A Checklist for Battle

Media-based Attacks

1. See if your software can handle a full storage medium. Fill up the hard drive and then force the software to perform file operations (by opening, moving, and saving files).

2. See if the software can gracefully deal with a busy file system. Some applications don't have the proper timeout/waiting mechanisms, so they can fail when the file system is busy serving a request from another application. Force the software to perform file operations in conjunction with background applications that are also performing file operations.

3. Try forcing the software through file operations with a damaged medium. Applications with weak fault handling code will often fail in this scenario.

File-based Attacks

4. Try assigning invalid file names to the application's data files, temporary files, and read-only files. Then force the software to use those files.

5. Change the access permissions of the application's data files. User permissions and read-write-execute-delete permissions are often ignored by developers.

6. See if the software can handle corrupt data in a file. Since most data corruption results in a failed cyclical redundancy check, Canned HEAT is the perfect mechanism to inject such faults. Otherwise, use a hex/text editor to change the contents of a file and then force the software to open the file or read from it.

■■ Summary and Conclusion

Testing the file system interface is often overlooked either because its inputs are hard to determine or because software is often deemed trustworthy when accessing files. Although the former is true, the latter is risky: software can and does fail when interacting with the file system.

This chapter discussed methods to test the file system interface and introduced Canned HEAT (which can be found on the companion CD) to make the file system interface accessible and testable.

It is important to test inputs from the file system. Such testing can reveal important failures and help testers identify potential file system risks for software that is released into a storage-restricted or otherwise unpredictable environment.

■■ Exercises

Professional testers can use whatever software application they are currently working on to perform these exercises. Students can choose any application they use frequently. At Florida Tech, we choose an application in advance for our semester-long class and everyone in the class works on it, usually in teams of two.

Once you have selected your test application, perform the following exercises. Just for fun, we'll refer to the application under test as the "target."

1. Pretend you are a user and use your target application. Make a table of features and list which features cause the software to go to disk or access the file system.

2. Install Canned HEAT and familiarize yourself with its operation.

3. Apply each of the media-based attacks to your application. Document the attacks that you applied, the features that worked as specified, and the bugs you found.

4. Apply each of the file-based attacks to your application. Document the attacks that you applied, the features that worked as specified, and the bugs you found.

CHAPTER 5
Testing from the Software/OS Interface

01100101011010001010100

Attacking Software from Software Interfaces

The applications we test usually communicate with other software systems. The interfaces over which this communication takes place are APIs (see the glossary for a more descriptive discussion under the terms "API" and "Interface"). We say, for example, that our application is "making API calls" to a network driver or to the operating system. These software resources, in turn, pass back data and return codes to our application. These data and return values are inputs to our application and must be validated, just like input from a human user delivered through a GUI.

The communication between an application and its software environment occurs automatically as we apply the UI tests discussed in Chapters 2 and 3. However, the UI attacks mostly force only "normal" software-to-software behaviors to be tested. Software developers and testers must also prepare for abnormal behaviors.

Developers have to consider that software resources can behave unexpectedly or fail. For example, a call to the OS kernel to allocate memory can fail if other applications are using all available memory. Furthermore, the memory-allocation routine could be buggy—it is software after all. If developers neglect to program error-checking and correcting code, it is our job to discover this during testing and ensure that it gets reported.

This is an enormous task. As we discussed in Chapter 1, the communication that occurs between an application and its software users is orders of magnitude more voluminous than human user input. Furthermore, understanding what APIs are called—and what those APIs actually do—is a daunting task. Indeed, take the simple case of memory allocation. How can we force a memory call to fail? It seems imprecise to simply run dozens of background applications, hoping that a failure scenario will occur. If we do break our application in this manner, will the failure reproduce? How will our developers diagnose and fix such a problem when told, "If you run forty background applications, sometimes our software hangs"?

Fortunately, a large subset of the activity between software systems is innocuous, which greatly narrows our field of interest as software testers. In addition, tools are available for identifying interesting aspects of software-to-software communication and exposing them to our test cases. These tools also provide mechanisms to inject specific faults into such communication, making testing of these interfaces more exact and repeatable.

Thus we frame the discussion of software-interface testing issues around the use of a tool designed specifically to carry out such attacks: HEAT, the Hostile Environment Application Tester. If you have yet to use Canned HEAT, first read Appendixes A and B.

Record-and-Simulate Attacks

The ultimate question for fault injection is, "What faults should we inject?" The answers to this question are varied.

Inject faults that cause all error-handling code to be executed and exceptions to be tripped

This is a very developer-centric answer. Indeed, it is an obvious goal to execute all source code, and it is common knowledge that source code that goes unexecuted before release makes error cases. However, aligning fault-injection techniques with specific source statements requires access to the source code and use of sophisticated code-coverage tools that must often be compiled into the application at build time. Unfortunately, source-based (or "white box") testing issues are beyond the scope of this book. However, don't feel too left out. Very little is known about systematic code coverage using fault injection.

Inject faults that can be readily staged in the testing lab

This is the typical tester-centric answer, and it is hard to imagine how one could be required to do more. Indeed, if the scenario you want to stage can't be done in the testing lab, how can you be expected to accomplish it? The problem with testing labs is that they are not representative of the real world. Users have more data, more machines, bigger networks, more software, and a wider variety of hardware, peripherals, and drivers than you have in your testing lab. Thus, users have the potential to generate scenarios that cause error cases to be executed and to find error cases that developers did not anticipate. The ability to stage a faulty environment is all well and good, but we need to stage environments that represent real user scenarios. This brings us to the next answer, which is the one we'll deal with using Canned HEAT.

Inject faults that might realistically occur in the field

This is the typical user-centric answer. Users expect your software to work with their environment. If they use a narrow-band network connection, your application should deal with it. If they use third-party applications that leak memory and your application is the one that fails because of it, they will place the blame squarely on your company for producing bad software. If they start ten downloads at once, we have little choice but to limp along the best we can.

The problem is that we can't control our users. Therefore, our application must deal with users and their unpredictable ways. Although we can't anticipate users' every whim, Canned HEAT's purpose is to deal with the most prevalent problems in an easy-to-use way.

Canned HEAT works on a simple premise: Behind every faulty environment are digital symptoms that we can recognize and recreate. Take a downed network for example. An unplugged cable, a misconfigured adaptor, faulty network software, network APIs that another application is using, or network congestion can cause this problem. However, the symptom that our application sees is that certain APIs for the network port are failing. Instead of working as expected, they are passing back failure codes to our application. Thus any number of actual faults end up producing the same symptoms.

Canned HEAT reproduces these symptoms so that the application thinks the fault has occurred. However, there is no actual fault to be staged. The simulation simply reproduces symptoms, and the software is none the wiser. Canned HEAT was built on a "record-and-simulate" strategy. We staged the faulty scenario, recorded the symptoms that the application would see, and created Canned HEAT to simulate these symptoms without having to restage the actual fault.

Besides the file system (described in the previous chapter), Canned HEAT simulates two of the most common types of software-to-software interoperability problems that testers (and users) run across: memory faults and network faults.

Memory Faults

The memory that an application uses varies according to the task it performs. Some tasks require very little memory and are unlikely to cause memory to be depleted or misused. Other tasks consume vast amounts of memory. Couple this activity with other applications running on the user's machine, and memory could become low enough for your application to run out of this crucial resource.

Canned HEAT is equipped with a memory monitor so you can watch your application's use of memory while it is running. If you put your application through its paces under Canned HEAT, you can easily use the monitor to determine which features are memory hogs. Fault injecting the memory-intensive features is generally more productive.

Once you have a list of memory-intensive functions, the first tests are to continually lower the available-memory threshold to determine where (or if) the application falters. You can do this in Canned HEAT by using the slider bar under the "Memory" tab and moving it incrementally toward the left until memory is depleted. As you decrease the available memory using the slider bar, force your application to use the memory-intensive functions on your list. Keep a pen and paper handy to write down your application's reactions to these faults. These notes may turn out to be good bug reports.

When you have determined your application's tolerance for low memory, the next step is to run scenarios that will test its reactions to varying memory conditions. Canned HEAT has a facility to randomly vary the amount of memory available to an application. The intent is to simulate the real-world scenario in which background applications access memory at irregular times. This background traffic will cause temporary delays in memory access and occasional failure of memory calls.

When this scenario is selected in Canned HEAT (by using the drop-down menu control just above the slider bar), available memory will be reduced. It will expand automatically without the need to run any background applications. You can then run your application through its paces, concentrating on the memory-intensive features identified earlier. Obviously, you should document all crashes and unacceptable wait times and report them.

The final test to perform is fault injection. The check boxes below the memory slider bar in Canned HEAT correspond to a different fault that we have staged and recorded. In general, we recommend injecting only one fault at a time. Whenever two boxes are checked simultaneously, both faults will occur, and developers will have a difficult time figuring out which fault caused the failure.

Performing fault injection with Canned HEAT is simple. Begin with the first fault, check its box, and exercise the application so the memory-intensive features are performed. Repeat these tests with each check box. I have yet to see an application that doesn't fail when subjected to this rough treatment.

Consider the following example using Microsoft Internet Explorer.

Step 1. Use the application to determine which features are memory hogs

This step can be performed while you execute the UI attacks of Chapter 2. Simply launch the application under Canned HEAT and pay close attention to the memory monitor while you use the application. Note which features use the most memory. Obviously, disk-intensive operations like reading and writing files will cause memory to be used, but loading rich images, processing large files, and performing any computationally intense function will also require memory usage.

Step 2. Determine the application's lower-bound threshold of tolerance for low memory
Once you have noted the features that use the most memory, see
how the application fares with restricted memory resources. You can
accomplish this by forcing the application to exercise these features while
simultaneously using Canned HEAT to restrict the application's access to
the resources that these features use. In this case, the resource in question
is memory.

Canned HEAT has a convenient slider bar under the "Memory" tab for
this purpose. Simply slide the bar to the left and note the decrease in main
memory available to the application under test (see Fig. 5.1).

FIGURE 5.1

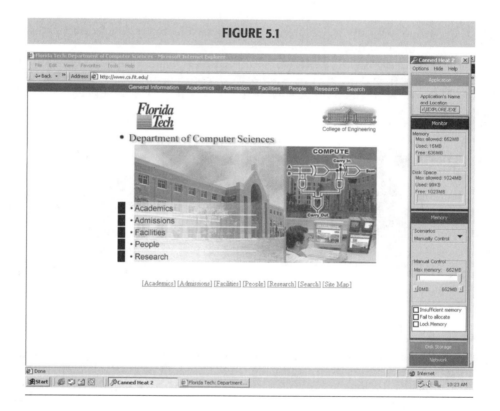

Note the slider bar is all the way to the right, allowing the application
access to all available memory. However, if we move it to the left and continue to use IE's memory-intensive features, note that around 35MB, things
slow tremendously. Furthermore, if we take away all but about 15MB, IE
ceases to work.

Step 3. Run Canned HEAT's scenarios that randomly vary available memory

IE's lower threshold for working well is about 35MB. This isn't bad according to the comparison tests I have performed on other applications. Once this is determined and reported to development, the next tests concern the application's ability to perform well under wildly varying memory conditions. Indeed, this is a much more realistic scenario because memory is used or it isn't. Thus it is reasonable to expect that an application will have enough memory or it will not.

Canned HEAT is programmed to simulate this dichotomy of resource availability automatically, using the "Varying Memory" scenario. Note that selecting the "Varying Memory" scenario will make the memory-control slider unavailable, meaning that Canned HEAT has assumed control of when and how much memory will be available for any request that the application under test makes.

Using this scenario will often crash applications even when you are not using them because any memory call could result in Canned HEAT injecting an artificial failure. Such is the case with IE as seen in Fig. 5.2.

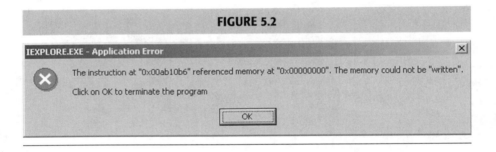

FIGURE 5.2

IEXPLORE.EXE - Application Error

The instruction at "0x00ab10b6" referenced memory at "0x00000000". The memory could not be "written".

Click on OK to terminate the program

OK

Step 4. Inject faults at runtime during memory use

The last test is to inject specific faults. Whereas the previous two steps simply fail memory calls according to the amount of available memory, fault injection allows more specific faults to be injected, regardless of the amount of memory available to the application under test. Note that these tests should be performed with the "Manual" scenario selected and the slider bar all the way to the right.

Figs. 5.3, 5.4, and 5.5 show such a fault in IE. We use Canned HEAT to simulate an "insufficient memory" fault and watch as IE's controls simply disappear due to inadequate memory resources. Eventually, IE will hang.

FIGURE 5.3

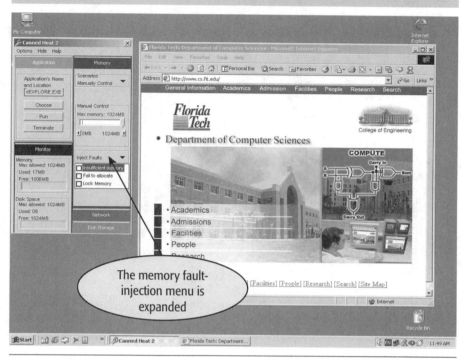

The memory fault-injection menu is expanded

FIGURE 5.4

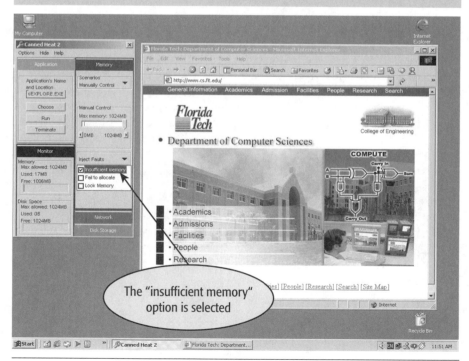

The "insufficient memory" option is selected

FIGURE 5.5

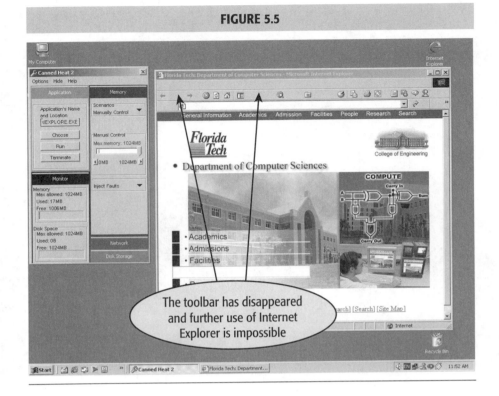

The toolbar has disappeared and further use of Internet Explorer is impossible

Network Faults

We test network faults with the same four-stage process we used for memory faults. First, we will use the application and determine which features cause network activity. Second, we will use Canned HEAT's slider bar to slow the network until our application is unacceptably slow, it crashes, or it hangs. Third, we will run network scenarios that vary the speed over time, concentrating on those features that cause the most network activity. Fourth, we will inject specific faults and force the application to use the network in a faulty state.

Let's consider an example, once again using Microsoft Internet Explorer.

Step 1. Use the application and determine when it hits the network port

Obviously, a browser's use of the network port (and thereby, network APIs) will occur whenever new URLs are opened, documents are downloaded, or components of a Web page are served to the browser by a remote server.

Step 2. Determine the application's lower-bound threshold of tolerance for a slow network

Once you have determined when the application hits the network port, it is interesting to find out the behavior of the application when reducing the network speed. This is done by using the application (for example, Internet Explorer) while manually reducing the network speed with Canned HEAT.

You can control manually the network speed with Canned HEAT the same way you can control the available memory. Using the slider bar, you can easily adjust the network speed to the desired percentage (see Fig. 5.6).

FIGURE 5.6

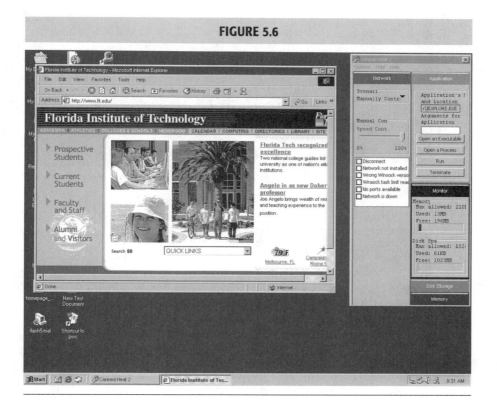

Figs. 5.7 and 5.8 demonstrate the use of the network slider. Fig. 5.7 shows a perfectly loaded page while the network speed is 33%. This shows that the loading of a page similar to this one does not require more than 33% of network speed.

FIGURE 5.7

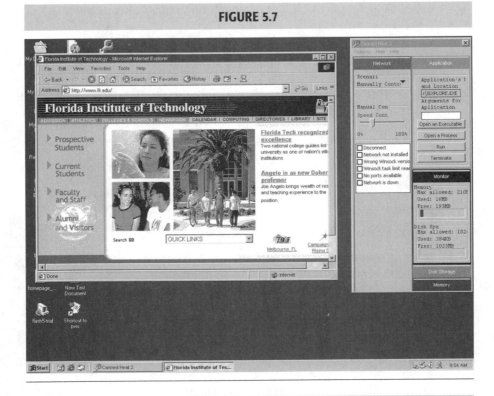

FIGURE 5.8

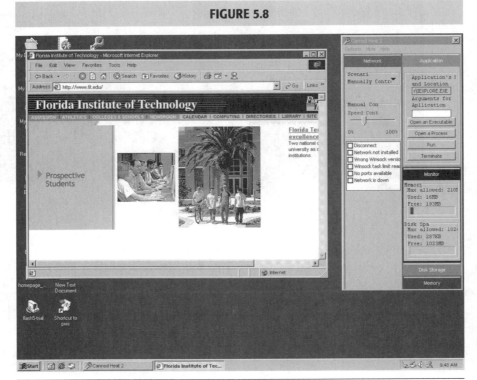

However, Fig. 5.8 shows an incomplete page (that is, some pictures and menu titles are missing) with a network speed around 30%.

We determined the network-speed threshold for which Internet Explorer cannot accurately load a page similar to the Florida Tech home page, with respect to the number of graphics, animation, and so forth. If we further lower the network speed, IE will stop working and will not even start loading a page.

Step 3. Run Canned HEAT's scenarios that randomly vary network speed
Once we have determined the network-speed threshold, the next step is to run tests using scenarios. In real-world situations, network failures are common. A scenario, especially one simulating random failures, definitely adds value to the testing process.

Canned HEAT is programmed to simulate random failures while the application is running. Examples of random failures are a down network or low memory. One can thus watch the application run while collecting data on the effect of diverse failures.

Fig. 5.9 demonstrates the use of the "Random Failures" scenario. Note that similar to the memory band, the network slider bar is unavailable when running specific scenarios.

FIGURE 5.9

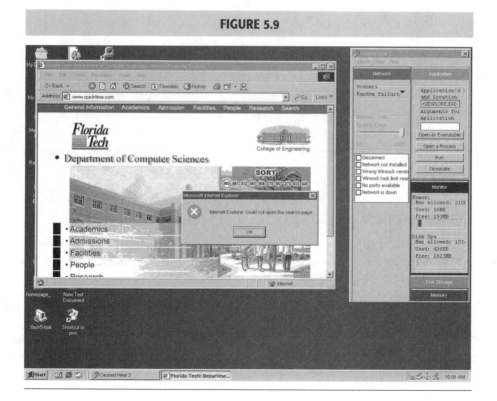

Step 4. Inject faults at runtime during network use

The last test is the injection of faults at runtime. The preceding step demonstrated the use of the "Random Failures" scenario. What we want here is to study the behavior of the application when inserting specific faults.

Canned HEAT allows inserting many faults including the "network is down" fault. When this fault is inserted, we can watch Internet Explorer's reaction to a down network (see Fig. 5.10).

FIGURE 5.10

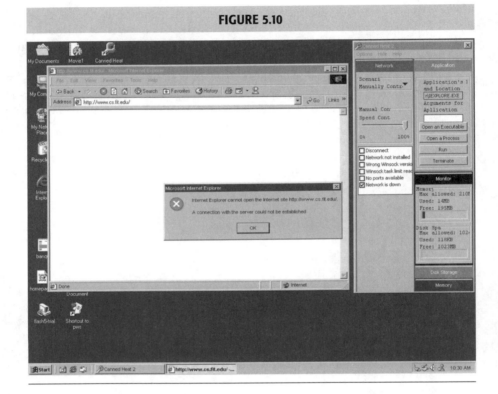

Observe-and-Fail Attacks

Canned HEAT is an easy-to-use tool to inject course-grained faults into an application's environment at runtime. It is not suitable when a fine-grained, surgical approach is needed.

Canned HEAT works by failing sets of API calls all of the time, most of the time, or some of the time. However, the tester has no ability to be more choosey than Canned HEAT's interface allows. Sometimes testers may want to fail a specific call only once, or they may want to fail a call only in very specific contexts. In other words, they need a tool to observe APIs being called while having the ability to intervene on a call-by-call basis. This type of fault injection is called *observe-and-fail*.

There are many companies that have in-house tools to do such fault injection, but they seldom release their tools to the general market. I will explain how to use these tools using a prototype we have developed at Florida Tech called Holodeck. Any *Star Trek*® fan will immediately recognize the holodeck as the virtual-reality grid where holographic images are indistinguishable from real people and objects. Holodeck is our code name for a tool that makes fake-software environments indistinguishable from real environments, from the software's point of view.

Similar to Canned HEAT, Holodeck can intercept API calls. Holodeck logs these calls so that testers can observe an application's activity and decide where to inject faults. Holodeck is equipped with filters that allow testers to narrow their search to very specific APIs.

Consider the following example, which represents a nice security exploit against the world's favorite Web browser. We use the target application and observe the system calls it makes, using Holodeck to view them. Most of these calls are mundane from a testing point of view, but some are not, and these can alert astute testers to possible attacks.

One such call is `LoadLibraryExW`. This call causes external-code libraries to be loaded for use. One particularly suspicious library is MSRATING.DLL, as shown in Fig. 5.11. We are alerted that this DLL is providing services to our application under test.

FIGURE 5.11

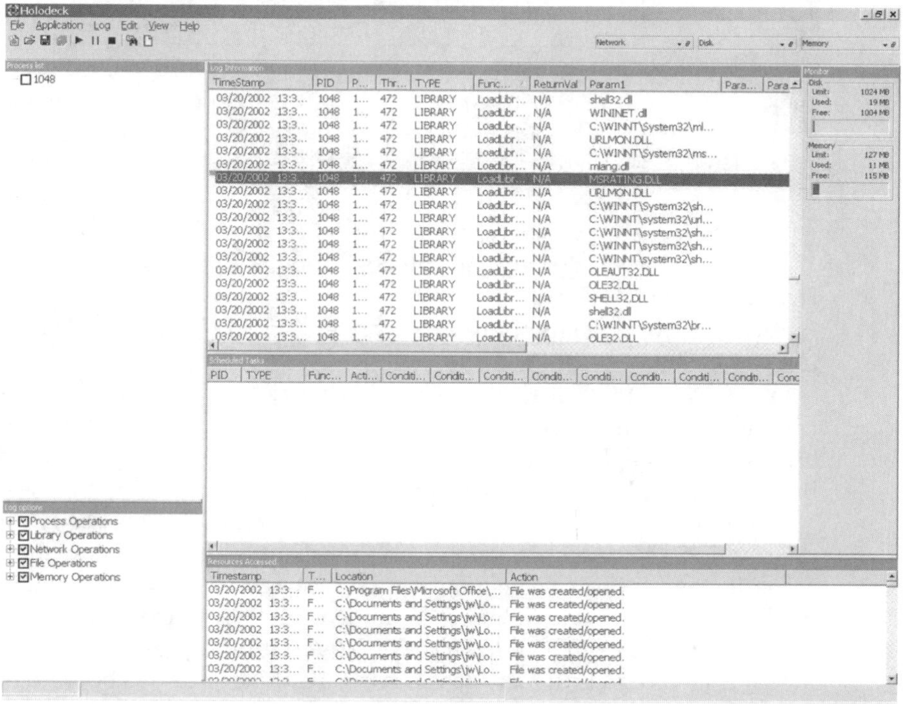

The desired behavior of the browser's rating system is to allow, for example, parents to set up passwords for sites so their children cannot access them. When the browser is pointed to such a site, it will prompt for the password, as shown in Fig. 5.12.

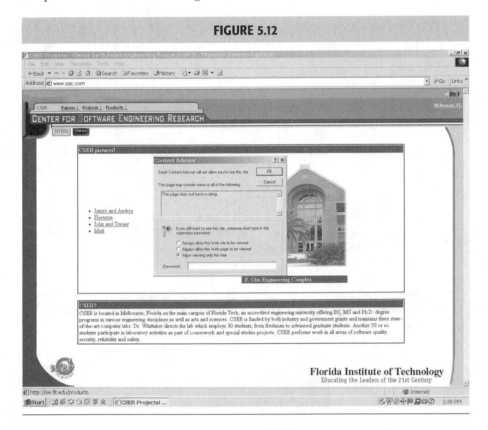

FIGURE 5.12

Now that the target system call has been identified, we can use Holodeck to inject a fault in the same manner as we used Canned HEAT. In this case, we will simply return a value indicating that the file MSRATING.DLL cannot be opened.

However, failing the call to `LoadLibraryExW` causes the feature to be disabled, allowing anyone to surf anywhere he wants. Note in Fig. 5.13, the blocked Web site loads and the rating options are unavailable, as indicated by the inaccessibility of their icons.

Holodeck is harder to use than Canned HEAT and is not ready for full distribution. However, a version of Holodeck capable of reproducing the scenarios in this book is included on the companion CD. Additionally, run-time fault injection with a tool like Canned HEAT is much better understood than is using a tool like Holodeck. Perhaps continuing research will change that and Holodeck will be released in future editions of this book or on *www.howtobreaksoftware.com*.

FIGURE 5.13

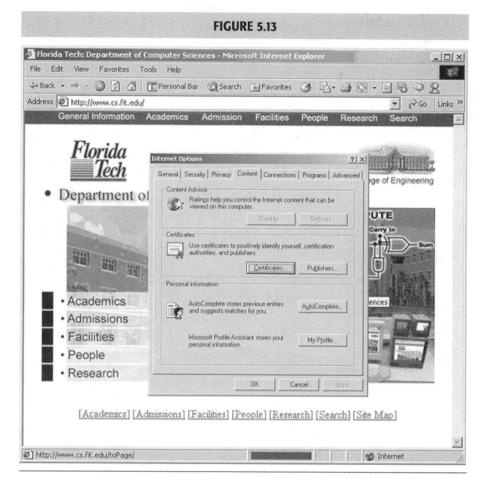

Summary of Software Attacks—A Checklist for Battle

Record-and-Simulate Attacks

This set of attacks requires that we stage a real fault and record the software's reaction to the fault. This reaction can be used to play back the fault for future tests. Fortunately, Canned HEAT is available on the CD, and this recording process has been done for you. All that's left is that you use Canned HEAT in creative ways to make your own application fail.

Observe-and-Fail Attacks

These attacks are much harder to pull off and are generally performed by product groups with very high reliability and robustness requirements. The idea is to observe low-level API and system-call activity, then individually fail calls by modifying return values and error codes.

■■ Conclusion

Be forewarned that with Canned HEAT, you will be able to crash just about any application on the market. However, just because you can crash your software does not always mean that you should. Testing software-to-software is a delicate affair. As we mentioned, most communication between software is benign and uninteresting. Thus it is sometimes like looking for a needle in a haystack to find the right set of API calls to fail. If your organization is not particularly quality minded or develops applications for which users are complacent about crashes, you will get little leverage reporting HEAT-related bugs. Get used to hearing things like "But that scenario would never occur in the real world."

However, if you work for a company that produces important software and words like *reliability* and *robustness* are in the common vocabulary, HEAT will be an invaluable tool. It puts within easy reach the input that is otherwise ignored during testing. Desktop applications that create important data—whose loss would be harmful to users—are good candidates for a battery of HEAT tests. Other good candidates are server applications, embedded systems, and any safety-critical or mission-critical application.

■■ Exercises

Professional testers can use whatever software application they are working on to perform these exercises. Students can choose any application they use frequently. At Florida Tech, we choose an application in advance for our semester-long class, and everyone in the class works on it, usually in teams of two.

Once you have selected your application under test, perform the following exercises. Just for fun, we'll refer to the application under test as the "target."

1. Install Canned HEAT and familiarize yourself with its operation.

2. Use Canned HEAT to launch your target application. Use the application and make a list of the functions that are memory hogs. Apply the fault scenarios listed under the "Memory" tab. Document the minimum threshold of memory for which your application can still function properly. Document how your application worked (or didn't work) for each of the memory scenarios. Make a list of the major memory-intensive features of your application. Use Canned HEAT's fault-injection mechanism to fault inject these features. Document the features that worked as specified and the bugs you found.

3. Use Canned HEAT to launch your target application. Use the application and make a list of the functions that access the network port. Apply the fault scenarios listed under the "Network" tab. Document the minimum bandwidth for network speed that your application can handle. Document the attacks that you applied, the features that worked as specified, and the bugs that you found. Fault inject each network-enabled function using Canned HEAT's fault-injection mechanism. If your application is not network-enabled, you'll have to find one that is to complete this exercise.

PART 4

Conclusion

CHAPTER 6
Some Parting Advice

01100101011011011000110100

You'll Never Know Everything

When you get your Bachelor's degree, you think you know everything.
When you get your Master's, you realize there are some things you don't know.
When you get your Ph.D., you finally realize just how little knowledge you
*   actually have.*

—*Popular saying among university professors, source unknown*

Knowledge is a strange thing. The less knowledge you have, the less you know about the vast amount of information that you have yet to learn. This is one of those "ignorance is bliss" situations. As you gain knowledge, you also gain insight into everything that you don't know. Having enough knowledge to realize your ignorance can be an enlightening and humbling experience. Being a tester for a long time is very much like studying for a Ph.D. No matter how much you learn, you realize that there is so much more to know.

This is what makes testing different from craft-based activities like carpentry, bricklaying, and so forth. I don't agree with those who call testing a craft. I do a lot of woodworking, and I rarely find that I can teach a master carpenter anything. Yet my students often teach me things about testing despite the fact that they are the apprentices and I am supposed to be the master. My conclusion is that testing is an intellectual endeavor and not part of arts and crafts.

So testing is not something anyone masters. Once you stop learning, your knowledge becomes obsolete very fast. Thus, to realize your testing potential, you must commit to continuous learning.

To this end, I have identified a couple of intellectual activities that we at Florida Tech use to stimulate thinking about testing. The attitude that I have tried to cultivate at Florida Tech is one of endless thinking and searching for answers to hard testing problems.

However, intellectual activities also require practice. So you'll see that the activities we perform are very much hands-on.

Bug Hunts

The first activity is the bug hunt. Bug hunts are held in our testing lab with two people per computer. These people are called participants, for obvious reasons. In addition to the participants, we have a referee, a recorder (who often simply wields a video camera), and a coach.

The participant's role is to apply attacks and test the application, specifically to find bugs. Bug hunts are exactly what they sound like—a direct attempt to break the software. Working in teams of two, one participant usually drives the application, and the other sits back and thinks about the big picture. The driver is in charge of pressing keys and navigating the application, and the back-seat driver is in charge of paying attention to the application as a whole and making recommendations about what to try. Often the back-seat driver is the one who notices when a bug occurs.

When a team finds a bug, they ring bells that we bought at an office-supply store. The bell is a really nice touch, and its sound is a tension breaker when it is heard, which is usually every few minutes. The bell summons the referee.

The referee acts as a judge. The bug is reproduced in front of the referee and judged to be a bug or not. The referee's word is absolute, and we often recruit three referees to ensure objectivity. Of course, when the bell rings and the bug won't reproduce, the offending participants are usually pummeled with boos.

The coach's role is to encourage the participants on to bigger and better bugs. In my role as coach I walk from team to team, reminding participants about attacks and pointing out things to try. Also, I steer teams away from unfruitful avenues of attack when I see them. Test leads and very experienced testers are perfect for the role of coach.

The recorder's role is as a documenter of the bugs and the situation that led up to the bug. Each bell ring brings the recorder, video camera in tow, to capture the reproduction of the bug and the participants' explanation. The video is often replayed later as a postgame analysis of technique, explanation, and yes, style.

We hold bug hunts immediately after a major new build occurs or a new feature is added. We generally limit the hunt to a specific area of the software. So we look for clues from developers about what features have had the most code modifications or new code added, and we target those.

The purpose of a hunt is not only to shake some good bugs out of a new build but also to foster teamwork and friendly, healthy competition among your testers. We always hand out cash prizes and try our best to bow to the victors when we pass them in the hallway. Winners usually get the "we're not worthy" bow for a couple of days after a hunt.

Bug hunts are always held under a strict time limit. We usually limit them to two hours. At the end of the two-hour period, the referee and coach examine each team's bug list and give prizes for best bug and most bugs.

Friday Afternoon Bug Fests

Anyone who knows the real James Whittaker knows of my love for socializing over food and drink. There is no better way to socialize than over a nice dinner. However, when there are too many people to converse over a quiet dinner, the next-best thing to improve service and keep the cost low is pizza.

We have a pizza parlor next to our campus called the Mighty Mushroom. At least once a week, my students, several other faculty, and I gather at the 'Shroom (as it is called locally) to talk about, you guessed it, bugs. We call these "bug fests." The goal of a bug fest is to learn by discussing bugs.

You see, I believe that bugs are corporate assets and that we can learn a great deal about how to improve our software by studying the very things that make our software need improvement.

Want to know what types of errors your programmers are making? Study their bug reports.

Want to know what testing techniques are finding the best bugs? Study bug reports.

Want to get new testers testing like your best veterans? Make them study bug reports.

Studying bug reports is boring you say? The report doesn't contain the insights you really need? I agree. That's exactly why we instituted bugs fests.

Bug fests are held using known bugs. If you hold the fests weekly, the best bugs from the prior week become the subjects of conversation. Here's how it works:

Monday morning send an e-mail reminding everyone to save the reproduction steps of their best bugs for the bug fest on Friday. Don't forget to make reservations at the pizza parlor.[1] Actual work doesn't change one iota. Everyone still finds bugs and enters them into the bug database. However, testers are challenged to become very familiar with reproducing their best bugs. Indeed, sometimes this very activity will help them find more serious side effects and create a better story to get their bug fixed.

On Friday we meet around noon. Testers bring their laptops, ready to demo, and developers are more than welcome to join, particularly if their bugs are part of the show. During the meal, we go around the table demonstrating bugs. By this time, testers have practiced the demo and have come up with some pretty good acting to increase suspense about when the application is going to go belly up. Often it is all in the sales presentation. Practicing bug demos like this is good preparation for writing a bug report.

---

[1] Some professional colleagues have bug fests at work to reduce travel time, which is always a good idea. However, I prefer to get people away from their offices, phones, and computers to get them to concentrate on contributing to the fest. Because the 'Shroom is an easy walk, it makes the perfect getaway for us. It's up to you to find the right spot for your group.

The better story you have about side effects and how this bug might occur will help ensure it gets fixed.

After each demo, we discuss the bug. Our mission is to get inside the head of the tester who found the bug. What were you thinking when you came up with this test case? What attack was being applied? Does this bug share characteristics with previously reported bugs? Are there similar bugs in the application that we might find? Could this bug be turned into a better bug? What are the side effects that this bug leaves behind? What user would run into this bug? How serious would the user view it? What did the developer do wrong to create the bug? Sometimes it takes twenty minutes or more to discuss a good bug.

Discussion is usually moderated, mostly by one of my senior graduate students or me, to make sure we stay on track and don't get too bogged down on unimportant details. I don't know how to teach anyone to moderate a discussion. A good book on the subject is [1]. Just play the discussion by ear and make sure the right information is conveyed. As long as people are learning, all is well.

Amazing things can happen during these discussions, and the ideas that surface expose new bugs and sometimes fundamental design flaws in the application. However, the goal is that everyone contribute some knowledge that then becomes a corporate asset, because it is shared and in the heads of more than one person. Indeed, the idea is for the novices to learn from the veterans and for the veterans to see novices, with a new perspective on the application, use it in ways they didn't realize.

As a finishing touch, we vote on the best bug presented and give prizes. Certainly, the presenter of the best bug doesn't pay for his or her lunch. Often they walk away with a trophy that travels week by week to the winner. Indeed, I know of a testing group that reverses this idea and gives an ugly, bright pink T-shirt to the person who submits the dumbest, most unfixable bug. The winner is only too happy to forfeit the prize the next week.

■■ Conclusion

Bug hunts and bug fests are great activities to encourage innovation, share best practices, improve morale and teamwork, and ensure that fun and learning are part of your job. I hope you are able to institute these and other such practices at your company. Testing should be challenging and fun at the same time. These types of activities are an important part of creating a good testing culture at your company or school.

■■ References

1. S. Kaner, *Facilitators' Guide to Participatory Decision Making,* Gabriola Island, BC, New Society Publishers, 1998.

2. C. Kaner and J. Bach, "Exploratory Testing in Pairs," *Proceedings of the Software Testing Analysis and Review (STAR) Conference,* pp. 622–628, Software Quality Engineering, Orlando, FL, May 2001.

Appendixes

Glossary

Annotated Glossary
of Programming Terms

API (Application Programming Interface): Software has two major interfaces. APIs allow software to communicate with other software, and GUIs allow software to communicate with humans. If your software has an API, it means people can write programs that can use your software directly. APIs are made of a number of functions and procedures (sometimes called *methods* in object-oriented speak) that perform various tasks. Although this makes using your application easier, it presents another interface that you have to test. Testing an API means writing programs that exercise the functions in the API. *See Chapter 1.*

Character Set: Because computers use binary numbers (that is, ones and zeros) to represent character data, each character is represented by a string of ones and zeros. In fact, every number, character, special character, and control character has a unique encoding of ones and zeros. Thus when you type the character "f", the computer sees the binary number that corresponds to that character. The ASCII character set is an example of such a character encoding. ASCII (American Standard Code for Information Interchange) was designed with only the English language in mind. It uses only one byte (eight bits, or a string of eight zeros and ones) to represent each character. Multibyte character encodings are necessary to represent all the possible characters of more complicated languages, like Japanese or Arabic. Perhaps the most popular multibyte encoding is UNICODE.

Computation: Software computes through simple mathematical expressions such as $c=a+b$. Software can compute with numbers, or it can compute by concatenating strings. Software computes things all the time, even when it is not directly solving a math problem. Whether it is fitting text onto a display area, calculating how long a user has been online, or adding new elements to a list, computation is something that all software does on a regular basis.

Control Structure: Computer programs are executed line by line from the beginning to the end of the program. A control structure allows programmers to change this sequence of instructions, allowing a program to branch to another instruction out of sequence. There are two types of control structures. *Branching* structures, like the if-then-else statement, allow conditional execution of certain lines of code. For example, for a user to enter a social security number, the programmer will often use a branching control structure to execute either error code (if the number is incorrect) or whatever code processes the number (if the number is correct). *Looping* structures, like the while-loop or for-loop, allow blocks of statements to be executed over and over. Developers might use a while-loop to read a file. In that case, the loop will execute code that reads a single line of the file over and over until the end of the file is reached.

Controls: *See User Interface Controls.*

Conventional versus Object-Oriented Programs: One can argue for hours to no good end about what object-oriented (OO) is. One can talk about a program being *object-based* and distinguish this from *object-oriented* (again to no good end), but testers usually don't need to be concerned about whether the program they are testing is objectified. OO is no mystery, it has never been new, and it presents no new black box testing challenges. At its core, OO is simply about how data and functionality are shared and used among a group of programs (see the glossary entry for *Data*). In conventional programs, data is stored locally within a program (so only that program can access it) or globally for all programs to access. In OO programs, data is stored so that it is accessed through a set of access programs. These access programs, and the data that they provide access to, are called an object. The benefit of OO is that objects protect data from other programs' misuse. The data attacks in Chapter 2 will test both conventional and OO programs and their use of data.

Data: This is information that a program stores. Data comes in as inputs from users and is stored internally in *data structures*. Explaining data structures takes an entire book for a thorough treatment. The most simple data structures are *integers* and *characters*, which store whole numbers and alphanumeric characters, respectively. There are more complex structures that allow groups of numbers and characters to be stored. Common data structures are floating-point numbers, arrays, strings, lists, stacks, queues, and pointers (which only point to other structures). Any data structure can be *global*, which means any program can access it, or *local*, which means only the program that defines it can use it.

Data Structures: *See Data.*

Delimiters and Fields (in a data file): Information stored in a file isn't simply written to the file in a jumble of bits. If it were, it would be very difficult to read back. Think of an address book. There are *fields* for name, address, zip code, and so forth. When the address book is properly formatted, it is easy to glance at the book to find a phone number because you know exactly where to look (that is, which field the number is stored in).

Address books are formatted for a human's easy reading. Files are formatted for a program's easy reading. Just as humans see the lines that separate fields in an address book, computers need to see when the name field ends and the address field begins. Thus developers use *delimiters* to accomplish this. Spaces, commas, semicolons, and the like are popular delimiters. Thus you might hear the phrase "a comma-delimited file." A line in the file would look something like this: Whittaker, 150 West University, Melbourne, FL. A program can then read the characters until the first comma and interpret that as the name, read the characters to the second comma and interpret that as the address, and so on.

Exception: *See Chapter 1,* Attack one. Sometimes errors occur that software is not programmed to prevent (either purposefully or neglectfully). When this occurs, an exception is "raised." Normally, programmers write code called *exception handlers* that attempt to make things right. For example, suppose your application tries to insert data into a data structure that is full of data. The runtime environment may raise a "data out of bounds" exception. If an exception handler is in place to handle this error, the exception handler will be called. If the developers failed to include exception-handling code for such an error, the application will crash, which means that the OS shuts it down.

Fields (in a data file): *See Delimiters and Fields.*

Files: Files are used to store *persistent* data. Files are better than data structures because they form permanent storage. Data structures only "live" while the program that defined them is running. Thus all data that is kept between executions of the software must be stored in files to be available the next time the application executes. Files are generally of two types. *Text* files are stored in native-text format. This means a text editor can read them, and humans can understand them. *Binary* files are stored in binary format, which is only machine-readable.

Input: This is an event that is generated outside an application that the application must react to in some fashion. Inputs can be keystrokes and mouse clicks, API calls, return codes, and so forth. *See Chapter 1.*

Interface: Software has many interfaces. The GUI (graphical user interface) is the most common and represents the interface between the application and its human users. The API is an interface that an application exposes to other programs. Suppose you write a set of programs to perform math operations. As a developer, you would write programs that will help your application get work done. If you wanted third-party developers to use any of these programs, you'd write your code in such a way to allow third-party applications to call these functions . This is called *exposing* or *exporting* an interface. The idea is that you are allowing other programs to make programmatic calls into your application. Of course, because you can export your software to other applications, you can also *import* the interfaces of appropriately developed software to access their internal functions. To illustrate this, think about Microsoft Office®. Excel exports its interface to worksheet functionality so that Word users can embed worksheets into a word processing document. Thus Word can import the interface to Excel without the user realizing that Excel is even being used.

Memory Leak: Programs often request memory to be allocated for their use *(see System Call)*. Whenever memory is allocated, it should be freed (returned to the OS) when it is no longer needed. A *memory leak* is a bug in which memory is allocated but never freed. Eventually, this bug will cause no more memory to be available. Good commercial tools exist to help testers detect memory leaks.

Object-Oriented Programming Paradigm: *See Conventional versus Object-Oriented Programs.*

Oracle: Whenever tests are run, testers must verify that the outputs the program generated were the outputs that were expected. Indeed, what good are tests that reveal bugs if testers do not notice the bugs? So testers must establish a mechanism that can compare the actual output that the application under test produces with the expected output. This mechanism is an *oracle*. Building an oracle is hard, and general-purpose oracles remain one of the biggest unsolved problems in software testing.

Output: This is an event that an application generates that is sent outside the application for further processing. An output can be a message printed on the screen, a string sent to a database, a request sent to the operating system, and so forth. *See Chapter 1.*

Paging: This term comes from computer architecture and gets to the heart of the difference between *memory* and *storage*. Both memory and storage can contain data that programs can read. Storage means permanence. Hard drives, floppy drives, and CD-ROMs are storage. If you turn off these mechanisms and turn them back on, the data is still there. Memory, on the other hand, is temporary. Each time you reboot your computer, memory is wiped clean. Although memory is temporary, it is much faster than storage. Thus when reading from a hard drive, the operating system will move more data into memory than is needed to speed up future data accesses. Paging is used to denote data being moved into or out of memory. You might hear the term *paged-in*, which means that the data has been moved into memory because a program needs it or might need it soon. You might hear the term *paged-out*, which means that the data has been in memory longer than useful and is moved to make room for new data.

Screen Refresh: Window contents often change. When users enter text into a window, the window must be updated to reflect the new data and any scrolling activity that took place. Users may also drag a window over another window, requiring that the entire screen be updated to reflect the window's new position. Updating window contents and the screen is referred to as *refreshing* or *repainting* the screen.

System Call: This is a request for services that a program makes to the operating system. Programs request such services as reserving memory to store data, establishing pointers to files, requesting date and time, and so forth. These requests of the operating system are collectively called *system calls. (See also API).*

System Input: Software receives many inputs from many different sources. One source is the local operating system. When a program makes system calls *(see System Call),* the answer to the request comes back to the program as an input. These inputs are *system input.*

Test Verification: *See Oracle.*

User Interface Controls: Human users communicate with applications via graphical user interfaces (GUIs). Applications receive input from humans through *controls* designed for the specific type of input being supplied. For example, if you want to enter text into a program, the program will present a control called a *text box* that is designed to received such information. If you want to tell a program to process text you've entered, *button controls* that accept mouse clicks would be the appropriate choice. There are far too many GUI controls to describe here, but some common controls are buttons, text boxes, list boxes, captions, spins, and drop-down menus.

APPENDIX A

Testing Exception and Error Cases
Using Runtime Fault Injection

Fault injection deals with the insertion or simulation of faults to test the robustness and fault tolerance of a software application [8]. Such measures are generally performed on software that is mission-critical, to the extent that failure could have significant negative ramifications. Actual injection of faults can be performed at compile time, when additional code is inserted to force error conditions to evaluate to true, or at runtime, when faults are injected into the software's execution environment. This appendix focuses on the latter type of fault injection and presents a new mechanism for inserting environmental faults. In addition, insight is provided into fault selection based on an analysis of runtime behavior. This appendix presents a methodology and tool for performing runtime fault injection, which is demonstrated on a commercial software product.

Introduction

For the purposes of our discussion of fault injection, code comes in two forms:

1. *Functional code* accomplishes the mission of the software by implementing user requirements. In other words, it is the code that does the work necessary for users to fulfill their purpose in using the software.

2. *Error-handling code* keeps the functional code from failing. Examples include code to check input for validity and code that ensures stored data does not exceed its defined type and value range.

By its very definition, functional code is readily accessible through the software's interface(s), be they graphical user interfaces or programming interfaces. In fact, testing functional code is a fairly well-established discipline, though often imprecise [9]. On the other hand, exercising error-handling code is generally trickier and may require more extreme measures. Of course, some error conditions are easy to handle; for example, some conditions require only that certain input values be entered incorrectly to be satisfied. However, different error-handling code may require considerably more complicated environmental circumstances to arise before it will execute [8].

Consider the case in which developers write code to guard against a full storage medium. The straightforward way to set up this anomaly is for testers to generate and maintain many data files that are large enough to fill the capacity of the local storage device. Not only are such files hard to generate, but keeping them means that the storage device can serve no other purpose (because it is full) than to house a single test case. Full media is only one case out of many faulty file-system possibilities. We also need to consider file corruption, access privileges (for example, read-only), file permissions, and damage to the actual media, among other scenarios.

Indeed, the file system is only one possible part of the environment that developers write error code against. We must also consider memory calls, network APIs, databases, third-party components and controls, and so forth. All these environmental elements can fail in ways that an application must expect and guard against, especially when its mission is compromised [10].

In this appendix, we discuss injecting faults into an application's environment at runtime to trigger failures in an effective, accurate, and manageable fashion. We begin by describing the runtime injection mechanism and provide specific examples for Microsoft's Windows operating system. Next, we discuss in detail the types of faults that can be injected and the situations in which testers should use specific failure scenarios. Finally, I illustrate the technique by outlining results from a case study.

A Mechanism for Runtime Fault Injection

Source-based fault injection can be complicated to achieve, but it is easy to explain: Source statements are modified so that specific faulty behavior is attained [1, 2, 5, 8]. When faults are injected to trigger exceptions, source statements are added so that internal data can be set to values that cause exception conditions to evaluate to true [8].

However, source-based fault injection requires access to source code and, in most cases, the cooperation of the original developers, which is not always a given [9]. Release pressure is one reason that developers refuse to write such code. Furthermore, many testers often have no access to the source code. Either they are outsourcers, or the build culture at their company does not support such involvement.

Regardless of the organizational factors that complicate source-based fault injection, runtime fault injection has the benefit that the faults are more realistic. By inserting faults into the environment instead of the application, the environment is freed of any additional code that may introduce unwanted behavior, and it is forced to react as if the failures were real and not triggered by testers.

Environmental faults can be forced by reproducing the causal scenario or by simulation. For example, consider the case of the ubiquitous network, through which many applications communicate with other applications or services. To test fault tolerance of network applications, one might physically damage the network by unplugging the cable or by sabotaging the network adapter. Furthermore, one could cause a busy network by generating large amounts of bogus traffic (for example, sending constant command-line pings from a few dozen machines).

However, these results and many others can be achieved by simulating the same circumstances so that the fault affects the application under test but not the rest of the system. The key is to realize that any environmental fault will manifest itself as failed system calls that the application makes. For example, the application sees a network outage as a series of failed calls made to the local socket API. The application sees low memory as failed calls to the kernel. The application sees file corruption as CRC errors that the function `CreateFile` raises.

Ultimately, there is the reality of a failure and the reality of what an application actually sees when the failure occurs. It is this latter entity that we can recreate, and it is at the system-application boundary that faults can be injected. These faults will affect only the system under test, allowing the machine to be useful for other purposes.

To understand how to interpret faults as failed system calls, we must first capture system calls before they reach their destination. Then we must record how real faults manifest themselves in the error codes and return values of these calls.

There are at least three ways to accomplish system-call interception:

1. *Source-based interception* requires editing of a binary and replacing instances of the destination API with an imposter API. The imposter X simply acts as a pass-through mechanism. For example, using a hex editor it is easy to search an executable for the string kernel32.dll and replace it with mykernel32.dll. We then write imposter functions in mykernel32.dll with the same name as the functions in kernel32.dll that we want to fail. The imposter functions simply log the call and then call the real function in kernel32.dll. When kernel32.dll responds to mykernel32.dll, the imposter simply passes the error codes and return values back to the application.

2. *In-route interception* can achieve the same effect as source-based interception without the need to change an application's binary image on disk. Using techniques published in [7], one can modify addresses in function-dispatch tables to divert calls to imposter functions. The imposters then act as pass-through mechanisms. Of course, in-route interception only works when calls are routed through a centralized function-dispatch mechanism like import address tables. Because these tables are stored in memory, the application's binary does not have to be modified on disk.

3. *Destination-based interception* requires inserting code into the function that the application calls. Unlike in-route interception, which modifies

memory addresses that are part of the application's code space, destination-based interception requires modifying the code space of the target function. In our implementation, we insert jump statements into the first few bytes of a function and copy those bytes to the imposter function. When the application makes the function call, the jump statement transfers control to the imposter function, which first executes its code and then transfers control back to the next executable memory location of the original function (that is, past our inserted jump statement).

Fig. A.1 illustrates the three types of interception.

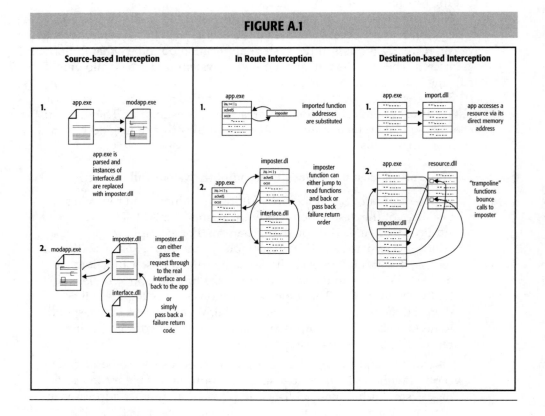

FIGURE A.1

Fault Selection

We have employed two types of fault-selection strategies and developed tools to carry out each type. The first strategy consists of recording function calls that an application makes and systematically failing each call wherever it is used in the application. We call this method systematic, call-based fault injection. For example, if we record that the kernel call `LocalLock` is used each time an application accesses a file, we can cause `LocalLock` to fail and force the software through paths that have file opens, reads, writes, and so forth, so that the application sees the failure of `LocalLock`. Obviously, this is a time-consuming, painstaking way to inject faults. The second strategy consists of staging a environmental fault, recording the pattern of failed function calls that the fault causes, and simulating that pattern in other parts of the application. We call this method *pattern-based fault injection*. For example, we might stage an unresponsive network by unplugging the Ethernet cable and recording that the application sees failed return code from any number of socket APIs. We can fail these same APIs as a simulated substitute for physically unplugging the Ethernet cable.

Pattern-based Fault Injection

The ultimate question for fault injection is, "What faults should be injected?" The answers to this question are varied.

The faults should collectively cause all the error code to be executed and exceptions to be tripped

This is a typical developer-centric answer. As desirable as it is to execute all the source code of an application under test, it is usually unachievable given today's relatively short development cycles and aggressive deadlines. Other difficulties include access to source code and use of sophisticated code-coverage tools. Again, not all testing teams have access to source code, development teams, or the required tools that would enable them to stage code-based fault injection.

Only faults that can be readily staged in the testing lab should be selected

This is a typical tester-centric answer. It may be hard for some to imagine that testers are required to run scenarios that cannot be accomplished outside the testing lab. However, testing labs are often not representative of the setup and environment of the real world. Users typically have more data, more machines, bigger networks, more software, and a wider variety of hardware, peripherals, and drivers than can be in a lab. Therefore users are a great source of realistic scenarios that developers may not have anticipated and that may cause unexpected failures.

Only faults that may realistically occur in the field need to be injected

Users expect that software will work well in their uncontrolled, generally unpredictable environments. However, because such environments are difficult or impossible to stage in the testing lab, we have developed a tool to simulate some of the more common faulty scenarios. We call the general principle the Hostile Environment Application Tester and the tool Canned HEAT. The purpose of Canned HEAT is to stage realistic problems in the environment in an easy-to-use way.

Canned HEAT works on a simple premise. Every faulty environment causes digital symptoms that the application recognizes and that we can recreate. For example, take a network that has gone down. An unplugged cable, a misconfigured adaptor, faulty network software, or network congestion can cause this. The application only recognizes the symptom that certain API calls (for example, to the network port) are failing. That is, instead of working as expected, they are returning failure codes to the application. Therefore any number of actual faults may produce the same symptoms. Canned HEAT reproduces these symptoms so that the application runs as if an actual failure has occurred.

Memory Faults

The memory that an application uses varies according to the task it performs. Some tasks require very little memory and are unlikely to cause it to be depleted. Other tasks consume vast amounts of memory. Such tasks, along with other applications running simultaneously, may deprive the application of the memory necessary for normal operation. To determine the features that are memory intensive, Canned HEAT is equipped with a monitor that keeps track of an application's memory use. Once a list of these features is gathered, the first tests continually lower the available-memory threshold to determine where (or if) the application falters.

The next step is to run scenarios that test the application's reactions to varying memory conditions. Canned HEAT can randomly vary the memory available to an application. The intent is to simulate the real-world scenario in which background applications access memory at sporadic times. The application is run through its paces, concentrating on the memory-intensive features identified earlier.

The final test is fault injection. With Canned HEAT this is as simple as running the application and selecting a fault's check box at any time.

Consider the following example using Microsoft Internet Explorer.

Step 1. Use the application and determine which features are memory intensive
This step can be performed while the application is being tested under ordinary circumstances. Simply launch the application under Canned HEAT and pay close attention to the memory monitor while you use the application. Note which features use the most memory. Obviously, disk-intensive operations like reading and writing files will cause memory to be used, but loading rich images, processing large files, and performing any computationally intense function will also require memory usage.

Step 2. Determine the application's lower-bound threshold of tolerance for low memory
See how the application fares with restricted memory resources. This can be accomplished by using Canned HEAT to force the features to be exercised while simultaneously restricting the application's access to memory resources.

Canned HEAT has a convenient slider bar under the "Memory" tab for this purpose. By simply sliding the bar to the left, the available main memory is decreased (see Fig. A.2).

FIGURE A.2

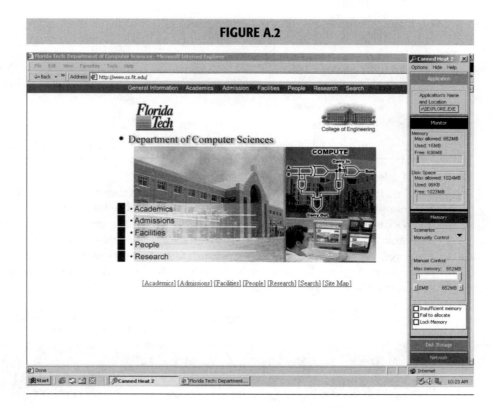

Note the slider bar is all the way to the right, allowing the application access to all available memory. However, if we move it to the left and continue to use Internet Explorer's memory-intensive features, we note that around 35MB, things slow tremendously. Furthermore, if we take away all but about 15MB, Internet Explorer ceases to work.

Step 3. Run Canned HEAT's scenarios that randomly vary available memory

Once this is determined and reported to development, the next tests concern the application's ability to perform well under tremendously varying memory conditions.

Selecting the "Varying Memory" scenario will make the memory-control slider unavailable, meaning that Canned HEAT has assumed control of when and how much memory will be available for any request that the application under test makes.

Using this scenario will often crash applications even when the human user is not working with them. This is because any memory call may result in Canned HEAT injecting an artificial failure. Such is the case with Internet Explorer, as shown in Fig. A.3.

FIGURE A.3

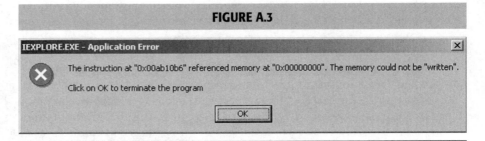

Step 4. Inject faults at runtime during memory use

The last tests inject specific faults. Whereas the previous two steps simply fail memory calls according to the amount of available memory, our tool allows individual faults to be injected regardless of the amount of memory available. Figs. A.4, A.5, and A.6 show an example of this in Internet Explorer. We use Canned HEAT to simulate an "insufficient memory" fault and watch as IE's controls simply disappear due to inadequate memory resources. Eventually, IE will hang.

FIGURE A.4

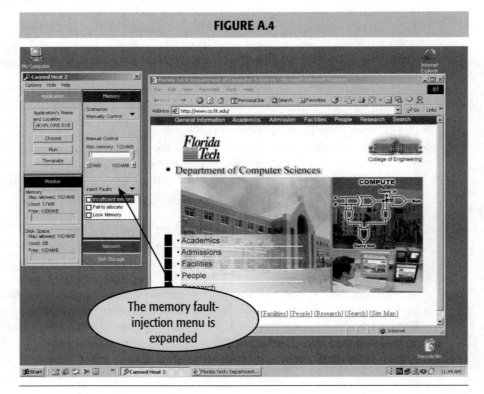

FIGURE A.5

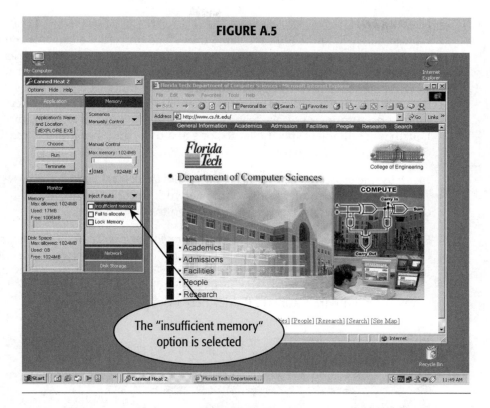

The "insufficient memory" option is selected

FIGURE A.6

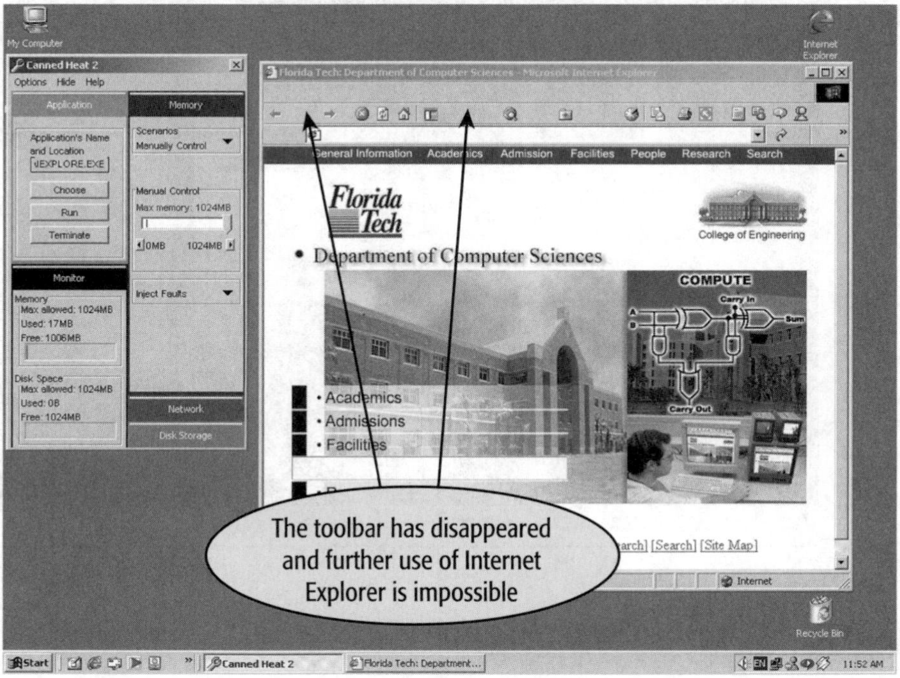

The toolbar has disappeared and further use of Internet Explorer is impossible

Network Faults

We test network faults with the same four-stage process we used for memory faults. First, we will use the application to determine which features cause network activity. Second, we will use Canned HEAT's slider bar to slow the network until our application is unacceptably slow, it crashes, or it hangs. Third, we will run scenarios that vary the network speed over time, concentrating on those features that cause the most network activity. Fourth, we will inject specific faults, one at a time, and monitor the application's resulting behavior.

Step 1. Use the application and determine when it hits the network port
The browser's most intense use of the network port occurs during file downloads and when Web pages are served to it.

Step 2. Determine the application's lower-bound threshold of tolerance for a slow network
Once you have determined when the application hits the network port, it is interesting to find out the behavior of the application by reducing network speed. This is done by using the application while manually reducing the network speed with Canned HEAT's network-speed slider bar.

FIGURE A.7

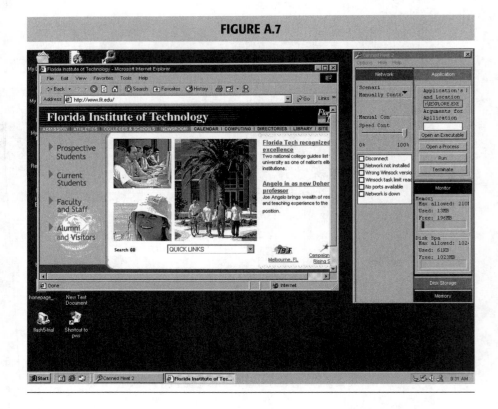

Canned HEAT allows the user to control the network speed in the same way it does for available memory. Using the slider bar, the user can easily adjust the network speed to the desired percentage of the full capacity of the machine on which the application is being tested (see Fig. A.7).

Figs. A.8 and A.9 demonstrate the use of the network slider bar. Fig. A.8 shows a perfectly loaded page while the network speed is 33% of its maximum. This shows that the loading of a page similar to this one does not require more than 33% of network speed.

FIGURE A.8

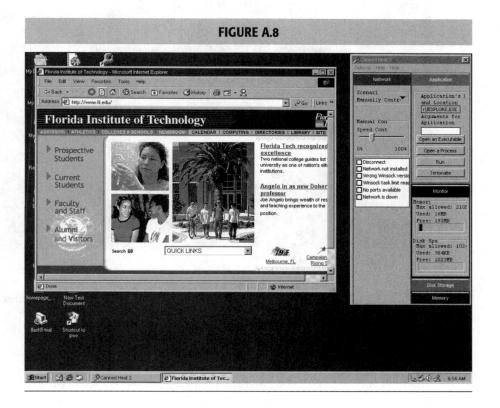

However, Fig. A.9 shows an incomplete page (that is, some pictures and menu titles are missing) with a network speed around 30%.

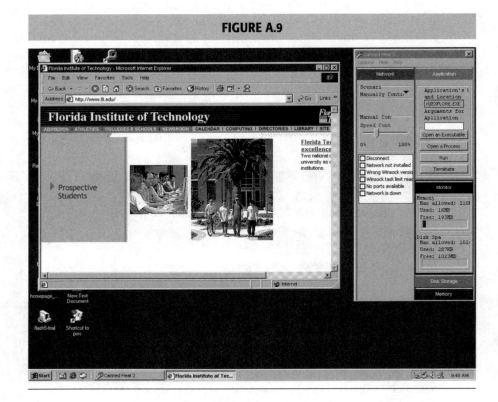

FIGURE A.9

We thus determined the network-speed threshold for which Internet Explorer can load accurately a page similar to the Florida Tech home page, with respect to graphics, animation, and so forth. If we further lower the network speed, IE will not be able to load a page.

Step 3. Run Canned HEAT's scenarios that randomly vary network speed
The next step is to run tests using scenarios. Canned HEAT is programmed to simulate random network failures while the application is running. Examples of such failures are a disabled network connection, an unresponsive network port, or a failure of socket APIs.

Fig. A.10 demonstrates Canned HEAT's "Random Failures" scenario. The network slider bar is unavailable when running random scenarios, as was the memory slider bar.

Step 4. Inject faults at runtime during network use
The last tests consist of injecting faults at runtime. The preceding step demonstrated the use of the "Random Failures" scenario. What we want here is to study the behavior of the application when inserting specific faults.

Canned HEAT allows inserting many faults, including the "network is down" fault. When this fault is inserted, we can watch Internet Explorer's reaction to a network that has become unresponsive (see Fig. A.11).

FIGURE A.10

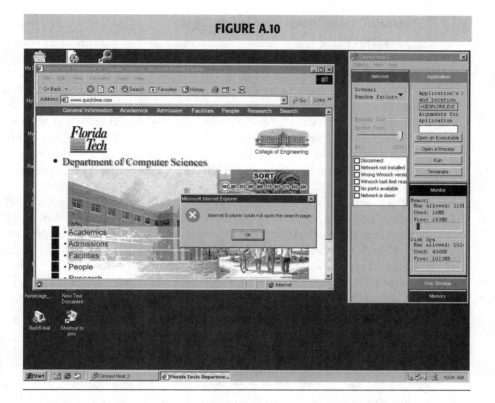

FIGURE A.11

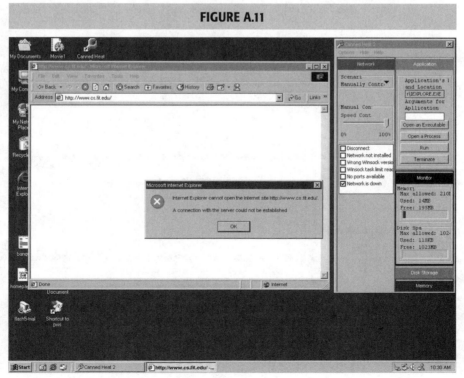

Systematic Call-based Fault Injection

Canned HEAT is an easy-to-use tool to inject course-grained faults into an application's environment at runtime. It is not suitable when a fine-grained, surgical approach is needed.

Canned HEAT works by failing sets of API calls all of the time, most of the time, or some of the time. However, the tester has no ability to be more choosey than Canned HEAT's interface allows. Sometimes testers may want to fail a specific call only once, or they may want to fail a call only in very specific contexts. In other words, they need a tool to observe APIs being called while having the ability to intervene on a call-by-call basis. This type of fault injection is called *observe-and-fail.*

There are many companies that have in house tools to do such fault injection, but they seldom release their tools to the general market. I will explain how to use these tools using a prototype we have developed at Florida Tech called Holodeck. Any *Star Trek* fan will immediately recognize the Holodeck as the virtual-reality grid where holograms are indistinguishable from real people. Holodeck is our code name for a tool that makes fake software environments indistinguishable from real environments, from the software's point of view.

FIGURE A.12

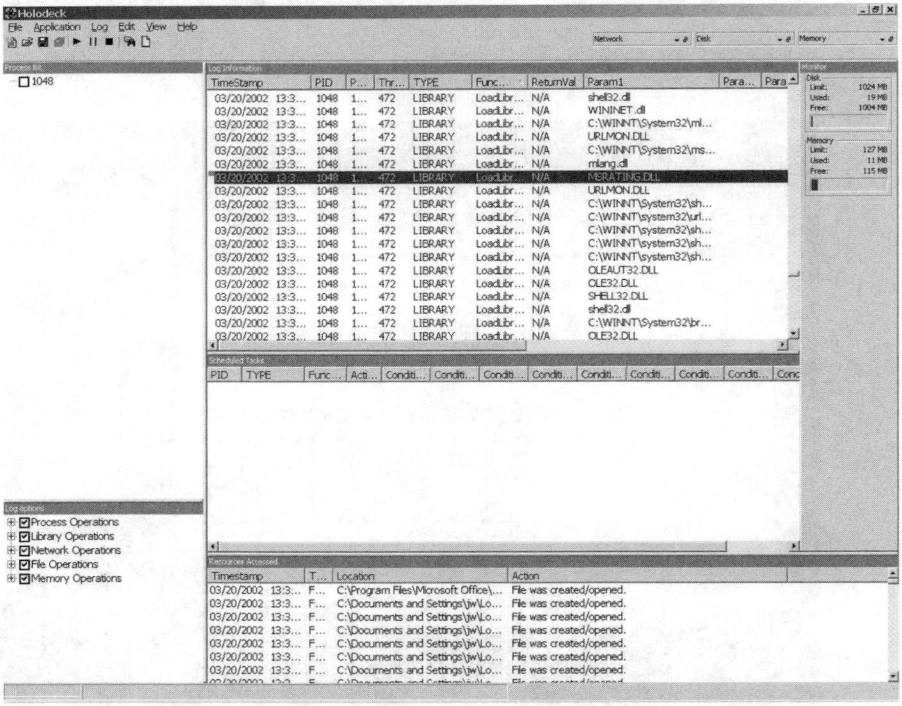

Similar to Canned HEAT, Holodeck can intercept API calls. Holodeck logs these calls so that testers can observe an application's activity and decide where to inject faults. Holodeck is equipped with filters that allow testers to narrow their search to very specific types of APIs. Consider the following example, which represents a nice security exploit against the world's favorite Web browser.

We use the target application and observe the system calls it makes, using Holodeck to view them. Most of these calls are mundane from a testing point of view, but some are not, and these can alert astute testers to possible attacks.

One such call is `LoadLibraryExW`. This call causes external-code libraries to be loaded for use. One particularly suspicious such library is MSRATING.DLL, as shown in Fig A.12. We are alerted that this DLL is providing services to our application under test.

The desired behavior of the browser's rating system is to allow, for example, parents to set up passwords for sites so their children cannot access them. When the browser is pointed to such a site, it will prompt for the password, as shown in Fig. A.13.

FIGURE A.13

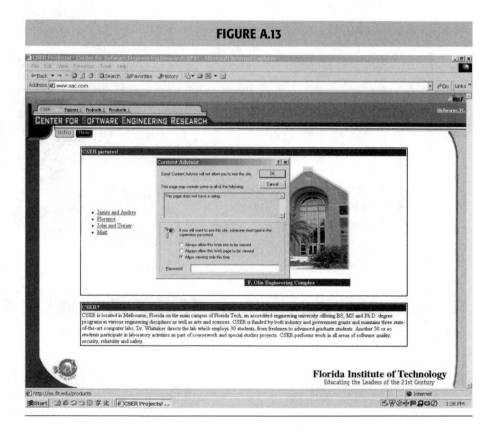

Now that the target system call has been identified, we can use Holodeck to inject a fault in the same manner as we used Canned HEAT. In this case, we will simply return a value indicating that the file MSRAT-ING.DLL cannot be opened.

However, failing the call to `LoadLibraryExW` causes the feature to be disabled, allowing anyone to surf anywhere he wants. Note in Fig. A.14, the blocked Web site loads and the rating options are unavailable, as indicated by the inaccessibility of their icons.

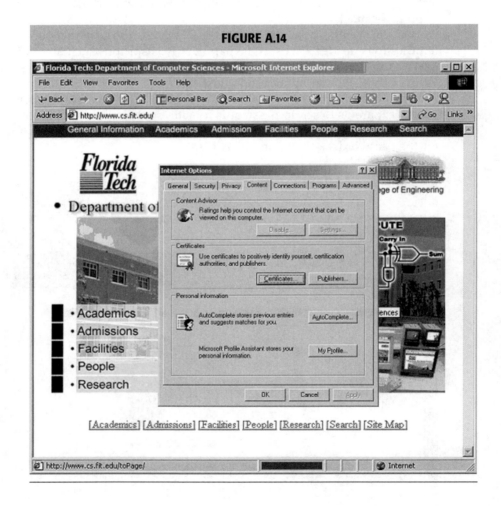

FIGURE A.14

■■ Conclusions

Triggering exceptions can be very difficult at runtime. Creating scenarios that cause exception handlers to execute often involves a faulty environment that is not easy to stage in a laboratory. Thus software is released without executing some exceptions or error-handling code. Because user environments represent more diverse usage than is easily reproduced in testing labs, these exceptions are more likely in the field. This predicament is risky for software publishers who must release untested exception handlers, particularly publishers who release mission-critical or safety-critical applications.

Runtime software fault injection allows faulty environments to be simulated in the testing laboratory. Performed judiciously, software testers can increase coverage of error-handling code and gain confidence in their software's ability to perform robustly in an unstable environment.

The tool and methodology presented in this appendix allow runtime fault injection to be performed without access to, or modification of, source code. By exposing system interfaces to interrogation, testers can reason about behaviors that may lead to exception handlers being executed. By modifying system-call return values and error codes dynamically, faults can be simulated so that the environmental fault is presented to the application under test in a realistic manner. This mechanism is completely general, allowing almost any type of stressed environment to be accurately simulated in a laboratory environment. As a result, the benefits can range from increased code coverage to a higher degree of confidence in the robustness of the application.

▪▪ Acknowledgments

This work was supported in part by separate grants from Microsoft Research and Rational Software Corporation. We thank the remaining members of the HEAT and Canned HEAT development teams, which include Rahul Chaturvedi, Andres De Vivanco, Aditya Kakrania, Terry Lentz, and John Brown. In addition, many thanks go to the testers at Microsoft and Rational for their insights into useful ways to fault inject. Special appreciation goes to Harry Robinson of Microsoft and Sam Guckenheimer of Rational for their input into Canned HEAT's user interface and fault-selection methods.

▪▪ References

1. Agrawal, H. et al, "Design of Mutant Operators for the C Programming Language," *Technical Report* SERC–TR–41–P, Software Engineering Research Center, Purdue University, West Lafayette, IN, March 1989.

2. J. Bowser, "Reference Manual for Ada Mutant Operators," *Technical Report* GIT–SERC–88/02, Department of Computer Science, Georgia Institute of Technology, Atlanta, GA, February 1988.

3. M. Friedman and J. Voas, *Software Assessment: Reliability, Safety, and Testability,* Wiley, 1995.

4. A. Ghosh and M. Schmid, "An Approach to Testing COTS Software for Robustness to Operating System Exceptions and Errors," *Proceedings of the Tenth International Symposium on Software Reliability Engineering,* Los Alamitos, CA, IEEE Computer Society Press, pp. 166–174, 1999.

5. P. Houlihan, "Targeted Software Fault Insertion," *Proceedings of STAR EAST 2001* (Software Testing Analysis and Review), Orlando, FL, Software Quality Engineering, 2001.

6. K. King and A. J. Offut, "A Fortran Language System for Mutation-based Software Testing," *Software Practice and Experience,* Vol. 21, No. 7, pp. 685–718, July 1991.

7. J. Richter, "Programming Applications for Microsoft Windows," Redmond, WA, Microsoft Press, 1997.

8. J. Voas and G. McGraw, "Software Fault Injection: Inoculating Programs against Errors," NY, Wiley, 1998.

9. J. Whittaker, "What Is Software Testing? And Why Is It So Hard?" *IEEE Software,* Vol. 17, No. 1, pp. 70–79, January-February 2000.

10. J. Whittaker, "Software's Invisible Users," *IEEE Software,* Vol. 18, No. 3, pp. 84–88, May-June 2001.

APPENDIX B

Using HEAT: The Hostile Environment Application Tester

Canned HEAT User Guide

Canned HEAT is launched as a 1.5-inch-wide window to be placed on the side of the application it is testing. This narrow profile allows testers to keep Canned HEAT and the application under test in easy view.

Canned HEAT consists of five bands that perform different functions. Depending on the type of tests run, the bands can be dragged within the narrow window so that any band can be obscured or viewed in full detail. Dragging the bands within the main window allows testers to switch easily between the functions of Canned HEAT as they are testing. It is very easy to get used to the Canned HEAT graphical user interface provided you spend a few minutes playing with the bands. Drag them and double-click them to get a feel for the versatility of this interface.

If you need to see all the bands, select the Expand All Bands item from the Options pull-down menu. Likewise, you can select the Collapse All Bands item from the same Options pull-down menu to get back to the standard window. In expanded mode, the bands can be combined (again by dragging) so that you can have any configuration of expanded and collapsed bands.

The Application Band

The application band allows you to select, run and terminate an application that you want to test. There are two ways of starting an application using Canned HEAT[1]:

1. The Application name text box allows you to type in the full path and file name of the application you want to test with Canned HEAT.

---

[1] This version of HEAT is limited to testing only normal executables and any libraries they invoke. It does not wrap Windows services.

2. The Open executable button allows you to select applications by
    browsing your hard drive. Clicking on the Open executable button
    causes the Open window to appear. Click the file format you want
    from the Files of type box. If you want to open an executable or DLL
    from a different folder, click a drive or folder in the Look in box of the
    Open window. To open a folder or drive in the folder list box, double-
    click on the folder.

Canned HEAT can also attach to a running process. To attach to a running
process, click on the Open Process button. The Process window displays
the process name and its process identification number (PID), along with
the path of the corresponding executable. You can select from the process
list by clicking on a process name and then hitting the Select button. The
Refresh button allows you to refresh the process list.

Once you have selected an application to test, click on the Run button
to launch the application. The Terminate button will terminate the application under test and kill any processes associated with it. The Terminate
button behaves in the same way as the Windows Task Manager in termi-
nating an application.

The Monitor Band

The monitor band displays the amount of memory and disk storage that
the application under test requests from the operating system. The monitor
band displays the maximum allowed, used, and free memory and disk
storage that the application under test allocates. Canned HEAT rounds the
amount of free memory and disk storage displayed on the screen to the
nearest byte or megabyte.

Fault-Injection Bands and Their Functionality

The Network, Disk Storage, and Memory bands constitute the fault-injection
bands. Each band supports certain common functionality.

1. The Scenarios drop-down combo box allows you to select manual
    control or a set of band-specific (memory, storage, or network)
    error conditions.

2. The manual-control slider allows you to restrict the band-specific
    resource available to the application under test. The manual-control
    slider can only be used when the manual-control scenario from the
    Scenario drop-down combo box is selected.

3. The Fault Injection check boxes allow you to inject specific faults into
    the application under test on an individual or combination basis.

The Network Band

The Network band allows you to simulate the following conditions.

Scenarios

The default scenario, set for the application under test in the Network band, is manual control, which enables the manual-control slider to control the amount of bandwidth available to the application under test. The manual-control slider is set to the 100% default mark. When the slider control is at 100%, Canned HEAT does not intervene in packet transmissions on the network port that the application under test uses. Sliding the bar to the left allows Canned HEAT to simulate a network slowdown by delaying packet transmission.

Canned HEAT simulates three other scenarios that duplicate the behavior of real network conditions that can appear in practice. For example, computer networks tend to gradually slow down as new users log on and initiate network traffic. The Gradual Slowdown scenario in Canned HEAT simulates a network slowdown by presenting the application under test with a slower and slower network as you test the application. The Erratic Speeds scenario simulates a network-fault pattern characterized by bursts of traffic and periods of full bandwidth. The Random Failures scenario randomly injects one of the network faults.

Network Faults

Enabling the following check boxes inserts network-oriented faults into the environment of the application under test:

1. Disconnect — Canned HEAT simulates the network becoming unavailable to the application under test. In a real environment, the network could become unavailable to an application due to an unplugged cable, software disconnection, downed server, or many other causes.

2. Uninstalled Network — Canned HEAT simulates a situation in which the computer has no ISP or network software installed.

3. Wrong Winsock Version — Injecting this fault simulates a condition in which the application under test runs on a computer that has older versions of Microsoft's Winsock API installed.

4. Winsock Task Limit Reached — This fault causes a failure that simulates the Winsock API reaching its full capacity in terms of the number of applications that have requested socket services.

5. Port Unavailable — Selecting this fault allows you to simulate a situation in which all available ports on a computer are busy, down, or otherwise unavailable.

6. Network Down — Canned HEAT allows you to simulate the problem of an out-of-service ISP, disabled router, or any other of the many reasons that a network could be down.

Disk Storage

The Disk Storage band represents failure of the file system as described in Chapter 3.

Scenarios

The default scenario for the application under test in the Disk Storage band is manual control. This allows you to use the manual-control slider bar to control the amount of disk space available to the application under test. When the slider control is at the 100% default mark, Canned HEAT will not intervene in file interactions of the application under test. Sliding the bar to the left allows Canned HEAT to restrict the amount of disk space accessible to the application under test.

Thus a small hard drive can easily be simulated by setting the slider control to the desired level. Canned HEAT will fail file-write operations when the application has used all available space. The Varying Free Space scenario causes a range of disk storage to be available to the application under test on a random basis. Random File Corruption randomly injects any of the disk-storage faults when the application under test makes use of the file system.

Disk Storage Faults

In the Disk Storage band, selecting the following check boxes will inject faults into the application's environment:

1. Insufficient Disk Space — Canned HEAT returns errors to the application under test, indicating that the application's attempted file writes did not succeed because the computer did not have enough free disk space to accommodate the write operations.

2. CRC Errors — Canned HEAT simulates file corruption of the application under test by returning an erroneous condition to the application stating that the cyclical redundancy check has failed on read or write file operations that the application attempted.

3. Too Many Files Open — This fault causes the file requests of the application under test to fail. An error is returned indicating that the system has too many files open.

4. Write Protected Disk — Injecting this fault causes Canned HEAT to inform the application under test that the media (that is, removable media like floppy disks or zip disks) is write protected.

5. No Disk in Drive — This fault is another failure related to removable media issues that Canned HEAT simulates, indicating that there is no disk in the drive.

Memory

The Memory band represents failure of the kernel as described in Chapter 4.

Scenarios

The default scenario set for the application under test in the Memory band is manual control. This allows you to use the manual-control slider bar to control the amount of memory available to the application under test. When the slider control is at the 100% default mark, Canned HEAT will not intervene in memory allocation of the application under test. Sliding the bar to the left allows Canned HEAT to restrict the amount of memory available to the application under test. Thus when the application requests more memory than the slider bar indicates, memory calls will fail.

The Varying Memory scenario simulates interoperability problems on a system where many applications may contend for memory resources. Thus memory may be plentiful one moment (when none of the applications need any memory) and scarce the next moment (when several applications make memory requests at the same time).

Memory Faults

In the Memory band, faults can be injected into the application under test by selecting the following check boxes:

1. Insufficient Memory — This fault causes Canned HEAT to return errors to the application when it makes memory allocation calls, indicating that there isn't enough memory available to fulfill the request.

2. Fail to Allocate — This fault causes the application under test to generate an error that can occur when memory is sufficiently fragmented or the computer is overly stressed.

3. Lock Memory — This fault simulates the failure of APIs intended to lock memory for the sole use of the application.

APPENDIX C

What Is Software Testing?
And Why Is It So Hard?

This was originally published in IEEE Software (Vol. 17, No. 1, pp. 70–79) and is reprinted with permission of the IEEE.

Software testing is arguably the least-understood part of the development process. This appendix explores the problems that software testers encounter and summarizes effective solutions. This appendix serves as an introduction to the subject of software testing and as a high-level, partial survey of existing testing technology.

Introduction

Anyone who has ever developed nontrivial software has experienced the frustration of users reporting bugs in their code. When this happens, a question always surfaces: "How did those bugs escape testing?"

Assuming that the software product is in error, the answer could be any of the following:

1. The user executed buggy code that we neglected to test. It isn't uncommon, because of time constraints, to release untested code. If the code is buggy, users can stumble upon those bugs. Compounding this situation is that even tested code can contain bugs. It is well known that covering source-code statements is no guarantee of failure-free software; the order in which statements are executed can determine whether software works as specified.

2. The user applied a combination of input values that were never tested. The number of possible input combinations is too large for testers to apply them all. Testers have to make tough decisions about which ones to test; sometimes we make the wrong decisions. Thousands of users can exercise billions of different input combinations across a software interface. A handful of testers cannot hope to check all these combinations before the software is released.

3. The user's operating environment was never tested. Either we knew about the environment and simply didn't have time to test it, or the user had a combination of hardware, peripherals, operating system, and applications that we didn't replicate in our testing lab. It is unlikely that companies who write networking software can create a thousand-node network in their testing lab. However, users can—and do—create such networks; the whole planet is their testing lab.

Thus testers must consider the software and the function it computes, the inputs and how they can be combined, and the environment in which the software will operate to plan and execute tests. This difficult, time-consuming process requires technical sophistication and proper planning. Testers must not only be good developers—testing often requires a great deal of coding—but also be knowledgeable in formal languages, graph theory, and algorithms. Indeed, creative testers have brought many related computing disciplines to bear on testing problems, often with impressive results.

However, the software-development industry still has a long way to go to improve its understanding of testing. This appendix presents a general model of the software testing process and discusses the problems that all software testers, regardless of their application domain, face. With hope, readers will gain an appreciation for the difficulties that software testing imposes on its practitioners.

The Software Testing Process

The sidebar *The Software Testing Problem* (on page 170) shows that even simple software produces many tough testing problems. To approach testing in an organized manner, I propose a four-phase software testing process. The phases provide a structure in which to group related testing problems.

1. Modeling the software's environment
2. Selecting test scenarios
3. Running and evaluating test scenarios
4. Measuring testing progress

Each phase has several associated problems that testers must solve before moving to the next phase. Each of these phases is discussed in detail. In particular, I focus on investigating the problems that testers face during each phase, identifying the technical issues that a proposed solution must address, and surveying existing classes of solutions used in practice.

Phase One: Modeling the Software's Environment

A tester's task is to simulate interaction between software and its environment. Such interaction occurs through an interface between the software and entities (for example, users) in the software's environment. Four of the most common interfaces that testers deal with are as follows:

1. Human interfaces include all common methods for humans communicating with software. The most prominent modern interface is the GUI, but older designs like the command-line interface and the menu-driven interface are still used. The inputs that one must consider are each mouse click, keyboard event, and input from devices that can stimulate the software. Testers have to organize this large set of input data to understand how it can be assembled into an effective test.

2. Software interfaces, called APIs (application programming interfaces), are how software uses an operating system, database, or other software application. The services that these applications provide are test inputs. The hard part is understanding unexpected services. For example, all developers expect the operating system to save files for them. What they neglect is the operating system informing them that the storage medium is full. However, even these messages are inputs to the software under test.

3. File-system interfaces exist whenever software reads or writes data to external files. Developers have to write lots of error-checking code to determine if the file contains appropriate data and formatting. Thus testers must build or generate files with content that is both legal and illegal. They must also create files that contain a variety of text and formatting.

4. Communication interfaces allow direct access to physical devices (for example, device drivers, controllers, and other embedded systems) and require the use of a communication protocol. Testers must generate both valid and invalid protocol streams to test such software. The commands and data, in the proper packet format, must be assembled and submitted to the software under test in many different combinations.

Testers must identify the interfaces that a software system uses and enumerate the inputs that can cross each of those interfaces. This is not always an easy endeavor, particularly considering the variety of file formats, communication protocols, and third-party APIs that must be studied. Testers must understand the interaction among users that falls outside the control of the software under test. Often such interaction can have serious consequences if the software is not prepared for it. I know of no complete list of things to check for, but some common examples are as follows:

1. The operating system user deletes a file that a human user has open. What will happen the next time the software tries to access that file?

2. A device is rebooted in the middle of a stream of communication. Will the software realize this and react properly or just hang?

3. Two software systems compete for duplicate services from an API. Will the API correctly service both?

Each application presents its own unique environment, and the number of user interactions to test can get quite large.

Another difficulty arises when an interface presents problems of infinite size or complexity. Specifically, two areas need close attention: selecting values for any variable input and choosing how inputs can be sequenced.

Assigning values to input variables consists of determining the values of individual variables and of assigning interesting combinations of values when a program accepts multiple variables as input. A technique called "boundary value partitioning" [5] is popular among testers to select single values for variables at or around "boundaries." For example, it is fairly well accepted that testing the minimum, maximum, and zero values for a signed integer is a good idea, as is testing values surrounding these "partitions" (for example, one and negative one, which surround the zero boundary). The values between boundaries are treated as though they are the same number; whether you use sixteen or sixteen thousand makes no difference to the software under test.

A more complex issue is choosing values for multiple variables that are processed simultaneously and could potentially affect one other. Testers must consider the entire cross product of value combinations. For two integers, we consider both positive, both negative, one positive, one zero, and so forth [6].

The latter problem, determining input ordering, is a sequence generation problem. Testers treat each physical input and abstract event as symbols in the alphabet of a formal language and define a model of the formal language, that is, a representation that describes how the symbols are combined to make syntactically valid words and sentences. These sentences are sequences of inputs that can be applied to the software under test. As an example, consider the input "Filemenu.Open," which invokes a file-selection dialogue box, "file name," which represents the selection (via mouse clicks, perhaps) of an existing file, and "ClickOpen" and "ClickCancel," which represent button presses. The sequence of "Filemenu.Open," "file name," "ClickOpen" is legal, along with many others. The sequence "ClickCancel" and "Filemenu.Open" is impossible because the cancel button cannot be pressed until the dialogue box has been invoked. The model of the formal language can distinguish the former as legal and the latter as impossible.

A model allows testers to visualize the entire set of possible tests, making it easier to judge how each test fits the big picture. The most pervasive model in practice is a *graph* or *state diagram*. There are many variations on the structure of the graph and the process of constructing it. Other popular models include regular expressions and grammars, which are tools from language theory. Other less-used models are stochastic processes and genetic algorithms.

We can represent legal uses of the file-selection dialogue with this regular expression:

```
Filemenu.Open filename* (ClickOpen | ClickCancel)
```

In this equation the * operator is the Kleene closure, indicating that "file-name" can occur zero or more times. This expression indicates that the first input received is "Filemenu.Open" followed by zero or more selections of a file name (performed through an abstracted combination of mouse clicks and keyboard entry), then either the "Open" or "Cancel" button is pressed. This simple model represents every combination of inputs that can happen, whether they make sense or not.

Now consider a model for the entire editor. We would need to represent sequences for the user interface and the operating system interface. Furthermore, a description of legal and corrupt files is required to investigate interaction with the file system. One can appreciate the liberal use of decomposition and abstraction to accomplish such a formidable task.

Phase Two: Selecting Test Scenarios

Many domain models and variable partitions represent an infinite number of test scenarios. To a testing organization, each scenario is time and money, and only a subset—sometimes a very small subset—can be applied in any realistic schedule. So how does a smart tester choose? Is seventeen a better integer than thirty–four? How many times should a file name be selected before pressing the "Open" button?

There are many possible ways to answer these questions, and lots of researchers are looking at the problem. However, the answer that gets the most attention usually relates to the *coverage* of some aspect of the source code or its input domain.

If one had to select a single buzz-phrase among testers, the word "coverage" would most likely be it. Testers strive for coverage. Covering code statements (that is, executing each source line at least once) and covering inputs (that is, applying each externally generated event) are the minimum criteria that testers use to judge the completeness of their work. Therefore many testers choose the test set that meets their coverage goals.

However, covering code and inputs is not enough. If it were, our industry would have very few bugs in released products. From the standpoint of the code, it isn't individual statements that are interesting but execution paths, a sequence of code statements that represents an execution of the software, that are intriguing. Unfortunately, there are an infinite number of these. From the standpoint of the input domain, it isn't the individual input that is interesting. Rather, *sequences of inputs*, which, taken as a whole, represent scenarios that the software must respond to, are most interesting. Again, testers lose. There are an infinite number of these too.

Test-selection criteria must sort through these infinite sets to determine the best set of tests for the money. Such criteria are referred to as *test data adequacy criteria,* meaning that they are an adequate representation of either of the infinite sets. There are many ways to define "adequate" and "best." Many testers want the set that will find the most bugs. We're talking volume here. Test management likes to quote numbers—the higher the better (high and low bug counts, and their interpretation, are discussed later in this appendix). Many users and quality-assurance professionals are interested in "typical use" scenarios, things that will occur most often in the field. Such testing ensures that major functionality works as specified and that the most frequently occurring bugs have been detected.

For example, consider again the text editor. If we want to test typical use, we would focus on editing and formatting because that's what real users do most. However, if we want to find bugs, a more likely place to look is in the hard-to-code features like figure drawing and table editing.

Test data adequacy criteria concentrate on either execution-path coverage or input-sequence coverage, but rarely both. The most common execution-path selection criteria focus on paths that cover the control structures. For example, testers might use the following criterion:

1. Select a set of tests that cause each source statement to be executed at least once.
2. Select a set of tests that cause each branching structure (for example, if, case, while, etc.) to be evaluated for each of its possible values.

However, control flow is only one aspect of the source code. What software does is move data from one location to another. The *data flow* family of test data adequacy criteria [8] describes coverage of this data. For example, testers might select a set of tests that cause each data structure to be initialized and subsequently used.

Finally, an interesting criterion that has received more attention from the research community than the industrial community is *fault seeding* [5]. In this method, errors are intentionally inserted (or seeded) into the source code, and test scenarios are designed to find those errors. The idea is that by finding seeded errors, the tester will also find real errors. Thus a criterion like the following is possible:

1. Select a set of tests that expose the seeded faults.
2. Input-domain coverage ranges from simple coverage of an interface to more complex statistical measurement.
3. Select a set of tests that contain each physical input.
4. Select a set of tests that cause each interface control (for example, window, menu, button, etc.) to be stimulated.

The *discrimination* criterion [12] requires random selection of input sequences until they statistically represent the entire input domain. So testers might use the following criterion:

1. Select a set of tests that have the same statistical properties as the entire input domain.

2.   Select a set of paths that a typical user is likely to execute.

Algorithms to select minimal test sets to satisfy each of these criteria are a major focus of activity for testing researchers. We'll revisit test data adequacy criteria in the fourth phase (test measurement) because it also serves as a measure of test completeness.

Most researchers would agree that the best criterion is difficult to determine and that it is prudent to use multiple criteria when making important release decisions. Experiments comparing test data adequacy criteria are necessary, and new criteria are needed. Testers should be aware which criteria are built into their methodology. They should also understand the inherent limitations of these criteria when they report results.

Phase Three: Running and Evaluating Test Scenarios

Once testers have identified which tests suit their needs, the next step is to convert the tests to executable form—often this form is code—and apply them to the system under test.

The key issue during this phase is automation. Testers often endeavor to automate as much of the application of test scenarios as possible. Applying test scenarios manually is labor intensive and error prone, a perfect forum for automation.

What testers are doing is writing code that simulates users. Complete automation requires simulation of the entire operational environment. Each input source and output destination that interacts with the system is substituted with a simulator[1]. Data-gathering code is often included in the simulated environment as "test hooks" or "asserts", and provides information about internal variables, object properties, and so forth. These hooks are removed when the software is released to the field, but during testing they provide valuable information that helps testers identify failures and isolate faults.

The second part of the execution phase is evaluation. The evaluation problem is easy to state but difficult to solve (much less automate) in practice. During evaluation the software's actual output (that is, the output resulting from executing a test scenario) is compared to its expected output, as documented by a specification. The specification is assumed to be correct, and deviations from it are *failures*. The entity that performs the comparison is called the *oracle* (see the sidebar *Testing Terminology*, on page 174, for an explanation of common testing terms).

However, in practice this comparison is difficult to achieve. Theoretically, the comparison to determine equivalency of two arbitrary, Turing-computable functions is unsolvable. Practically, imagine the text

---

[1] It is interesting to note that programs that simulate human users are often referred to as "monkeys," symbolic of training a monkey (the program) to do a human's (the tester's) job.

editor again. If the output is supposed to be "highlight a misspelled word," how can we determine that each instance of misspelling has been detected? This is why in most cases, the oracle is a human tester who visually monitors screen output and painstakingly analyzes output data.

The evaluation process remains the biggest unsolved problem for testing researchers. However, some help is available via two different mechanisms.

The first approach is through very hard work and formalism. Chiefly, this is done by formalizing the way specifications are written and the way designs and code are derived from them [7]. Both object-oriented and structured development contain mechanisms for formally expressing specifications to make the task of comparing expected and actual behavior easier. The industry as a whole has shied away from formal methods. However, do not underestimate the helpfulness of a good specification, even if it is informal. For readers who want to do something nice for their testers, write them a specification; without one, testers are likely to find only obvious bugs and miss the subtle ones. Furthermore, the absence of a specification wastes significant time when testers report unspecified features as bugs.

The second approach consists of embedding test code in the application under test. There are two possibilities for such test code. The simple case is that test code exposes certain internal data objects or states that make it easier for an external oracle to judge correctness. Such functionality is implemented without being visible to users. Testers can access test-code results programmatically (for example, a test API) or through a debugger. A more complex solution is to write programs in such a way that they are self-testing [3]. Sometimes this involves coding multiple solutions to the problem and having one solution check the other, or it might mean writing "inverse" routines that "undo" each operation. If an operation is performed and then "undone," the resulting software state should be equivalent to its state before the operation. In this situation the oracle is not perfect; there could be a bug in both operations where each bug masks the other.

The real issue for testers is that developers write code with testing in mind. If the code will be hard to test and verify, it should be rewritten to make it more testable. Likewise, a testing methodology should also be judged by its contribution to solving the automation and oracle problems. Too many methodologies provide little guidance in these areas.

Another tough issue that testers deal with while running and verifying tests is the coordination of debugging activity with developers. As failures are identified by testers and diagnosed by developers,[2] two issues arise: failure reproduction and test-scenario reexecution.

---

[2] My assumption here is that testers and developers are two distinct groups within a software organization or, at the very least, two distinct roles that any group or individual must play.

Failure reproduction is not the no-brainer it seems to be. The obvious answer is, of course, that you simply rerun the offending test and reobserve the errant behavior. However, anyone who has spent any time testing knows that just rerunning a test does not guarantee that the exact same conditions are created. Indeed, often one has to know the exact state of the operating system, other companion software (for example, client-server applications require reproduction of the conditions surrounding the client and server), test automation, peripheral devices, and any other background application running locally or over the network that could affect the application being tested. It's no wonder that one of the most common phrases you'll hear when you spend time in a testing shop is, "Well, it was behaving differently before."

Once a tester successfully reproduces a failure, it is submitted to development and, in general, a new *version* (one in which the bug has been supposedly removed) of the software is created. Testing progresses through a series of software versions until one is determined to be fit for release. A serious question arises out of this: How much retesting (called *regression testing*) of version *n* is necessary using the tests that were run against version *n*-1?

A specific fix can fix only the problem that was reported, fail to fix the problem, fix the problem but break something that was previously working, or fail to fix the problem *and* break something else. It seems that it would be prudent to rerun every test from version *n*-1 on version *n* before testing anything new. However, this is generally too expensive [9]. Besides that, new versions are often packed with new functionality in addition to the bug fixes, so the regression tests take time away from testing new code. Testers end up working closely with developers to prioritize and minimize regression tests to save resources.

Regression testing also affects the prior test-selection phase because selecting regression tests involves a temporary shift in the purpose of the test data adequacy criteria. When choosing regression tests, testers are only interested in tests that show the absence of a fault (or faults) and tests that force the application to exhibit specific behavior. The test data adequacy criteria that have heretofore guided test selection are ignored in favor of ensuring that a reliable fix to the code has been made.

Phase Four: Measuring Testing Progress

Let's say that I am a tester, and my manager asks a simple, direct question: "What's the status of your testing?" I call this "the question that all testers hate," because testers are often asked this question but are not well equipped to answer it.

The state of the practice in test measurement is to count things. We count the number of inputs we've applied, the percentage of code we've covered, the number of times we've invoked the application, the number of times we've terminated the application successfully, the number of failures we found, and so forth.

However, interpreting such counts is difficult. For example, is finding lots of failures good news or bad? Well, it could be either. A high bug count could mean that testing was thorough, and there are very few bugs remaining. However, it could mean that the software simply has lots of bugs, and even though a good number have been exposed, lots of them remain.

Counting tabulations yield very little insight into the progress of testing. Many testers augment this data with questions similar to the following lists to help them judge progress.

Structural completeness criteria:

1. Have I tested for common programming errors?
2. Have I exercised all the source code?
3. Have I forced all the internal data to be initialized and used?
4. Have I found all seeded errors?

Functional completeness criteria:

1. Have I thought through the ways in which the software can fail and selected tests that show it doesn't? [2]
2. Have I applied all the inputs? [5]
3. Have I completely explored the state space of the software? [12]
4. Have I run all the scenarios that I expect a user to execute? [4].

These are essentially test data adequacy criteria, and they are helpful to testers. However, determining when to stop testing is a deeper issue. What testers are interested in are quantitative measures of the number of bugs left in the software and the probability that these bugs will be discovered in the field. As is often the case in testing, there is both a structural and functional way of looking at this problem.

From a structural standpoint, an idea called *testability* [10] has been proposed as a way of determining the testing complexity of an application. The idea that the number of lines of code determines how hard software is to test is outdated; the issue is much cloudier than that. This is where testability comes into play. If a product has high testability, it is easy to test, and consequently, bugs are easier to find. One can monitor testing and observe that because bugs are becoming rarer, it is unlikely that many undiscovered ones exist. Low testability requires many more tests to draw the same conclusions; one would expect that bugs are harder to find. The idea of testability is compelling. However, it is in its infancy, and no real data on its predictive ability has been published.

From a functional standpoint, the use of *reliability* [4] is well established. *Reliability models* are mathematical models of test scenarios and failure data that attempt to predict future failure patterns based on past data.

In other words, they attempt to predict how software will behave in the field based on how it behaved during testing. To accomplish this, most reliability models require the specification of an *operational profile,* a description of how users are expected to apply input. To compute the probability of failure, these models make assumptions about the underlying probability distribution that governs the appearance rate of failures. Researchers and practitioners alike have expressed skepticism that such profiles can be accurately assembled. Furthermore, the assumptions of common reliability models have not been theoretically or experimentally verified except in specific application domains. Nevertheless, successful case studies have given this idea credibility.

▪▪ Conclusion

Software testing is a difficult endeavor that requires education, skill, practice, and experience. Building good testing strategies requires merging many different disciplines and techniques. Good theories exist that can help guide testers through the arduous tasks that constitute software testing.

▪▪ References

1. B. Beizer, *Software Testing Techniques,* New York, NY, Van Nostrand Reinhold, 1990.

2. J. B. Goodenough and S. L. Gerhard, "Toward a Theory of Test Data Selection," *IEEE Transactions on Software Engineering,* Vol. 2, No. 2, pp. 156–173, June 1975.

3. D. Knuth, "Literate Programming," *The Computer Journal,* Vol. 27, No. 2, pp. 97–111, May 1984.

4. J. D. Musa, "Software Reliability Engineered Testing," *IEEE Computer,* Vol. 29, No. 11, pp. 61–68, November 1996.

5. G. J. Myers, *The Art of Software Testing,* New York, NY, Wiley, 1979.

6. T. J. Ostand and M. J. Balcer, "The Category-Partition Technique for Specifying and Generating Functional Tests," *Communications of the ACM,* Vol. 31, No. 6, pp. 676–686, June 1988.

7. D. K. Peters and D. L. Parnas, "Using Test Oracles Generated from Program Documentation," *IEEE Transactions on Software Engineering,* Vol. 24, No. 3, pp. 161–173, March 1998.

8. S. Rapps and E. J. Weyuker, "Selecting Software Test Data Using Data Flow Information," *IEEE Transaction on Software Engineering,* Vol. 11, No. 4, pp. 367–375, April 1985.

9. G. Rothermel and M. J. Harrold, "A Safe, Efficient Algorithm for Regression Test Selection," *Proceedings of the IEEE Software Maintenance Conference,* pp. 358–367, 1993.

10. J. M. Voas, "PIE: A Dynamic Failure-based Technique," *IEEE Transactions on Software Engineering,* Vol. 18, No. 8, pp. 717-727, August 1992.

11. E. J. Weyuker and T. J. Ostrand, "Theories of Program Testing and the Application of Revealing Subdomains," *IEEE Transactions on Software Engineering,* Vol. 6, No. 3, pp. 236–246, May 1980.

12. J. A. Whittaker and M. G. Thomason, "A Markov Chain Model for Statistical Software Testing," *IEEE Transaction on Software Engineering,* Vol. 20, No. 10, pp. 812–824, October 1994.

The Software Testing Problem

Consider a small program that displays a window showing the current system time and date. The program allows the displays to be changed by typing new values into the edit fields as shown in Fig C.1. The program is terminated by supplying the alt-F4 keystroke sequence. The tab key moves between fields.

FIGURE C.1

Current Time: 9:28:32pm	New Time: _____
Current Date: 24 Aug 1999	New Date: _____

There are three things to consider when deciding how to test this, or any, software application: the environment in which the software operates, the source code that defines the software, and the interface between the software and its environment.

Environment

Software exists in an environment in which other entities, generally called users, stimulate it with inputs. The software then provides those users with output. It isn't readily apparent, but this example program has two input sources: the obvious human user who supplies inputs from the set, (for example, time, date, tab, alt-F4) and the operating system user that supplies memory for the program to run and the current system time and date as an application service.

A diligent tester will consider not only valid inputs from these sources but also invalid and unexpected ones as well. What if the human user types other alt-sequences or keystrokes outside the acceptable input set? What if available memory is insufficient for the program to run? What if the system clock is malfunctioning? Testers must consider all these possibilities, select the most important cases among them, and figure out how to simulate these conditions.

However, the job is not yet complete. After considering inputs from each individual source, testers think about how the users can interact with each other in ways that may cause the software to fail. What happens, for example, when another program changes the time and date? Does our application properly reflect this change? It isn't always easy to figure these situations out, but today's multitasking operating systems demand that testers think through such scenarios.

Source Code

The code for this application might have a "while" loop similar to the following:

```
Input = GetInput ()
While (Input ≠ Alt-F4) do
 Case (Input = Time)
   If ValidHour(Time.Hour) and ValidMin(Time.Minute) and
     ValidSec(Time.Second) and ValidAP(Time.AmPm)
   Then
     UpdateSystemTime(Time)
   Else
     DisplayError("Invalid Time.")
   Endif
 Case (Input = Date)
   If ValidMnth(Date.Day) and ValidDay(Date.Month) and
     ValidYear(Date.Year)
   Then
     UpdateSystemDate(Date)
   Else
     DisplayError("Invalid Date.")
   Endif
 Case (Input = Tab)
   If TabLocation = 1
   Then
     MoveCursor(2)
     TabLocation = 2
   Else
     MoveCursor(1)
     TabLocation = 1
   Endif
 Endcase
 Input = GetInput ()
Enddo
```

How many test cases does it take to cover the source code? The key to determining this is to evaluate each condition to both true and false. This way we execute not only each source statement, but we also cover each possible branch in the software. A tried-and-true tool for counting the number of tests required to achieve this is the *truth table*, which tracks the possible values of each condition.

The following truth table documents each possible combination of conditions in the "while" loop, the three parts of the "case" statement, and the nested "if" statements.

	While	Case 1	If 1	Case 2	If 2	Case 3	If 3
				TABLE C.1			
1	F	-	-	-	-	-	-
2	T	T	T	-	-	-	-
3	**T**	**T**	**F**	-	-	-	-
4	T	F	-	T	T	-	-
5	**T**	**F**	-	**T**	**F**	-	-
6	T	F	-	F	-	T	T
7	T	F	-	F	-	T	F
8	T	F	-	F	-	F	-

However, these eight possible cases only cover statements and branches. When we consider how each complex condition in the "if" statements actually is evaluated, we have to add several more cases. Although there is only one way for these statements to evaluate correctly (that is, every condition must be true for the statement to be true), there is more than one way for the first two "if" statements to evaluate incorrectly. In fact, we'd find that there are 2^x-1 (where x is the number of conditions in the statement) ways if we actually construct the truth table.

Using this logic, there are 2^4-1=15 ways to execute the third test and 2^3-1=7 ways to execute the fifth test (each of these cases appears in boldface in Table C.1 for reference), for a total of twenty-eight test cases. Now, imagine how many test cases would be required to test a modern software system with a few hundred thousand lines of code and thousands of such complex conditions to evaluate. It's easy to see why it is common to release software products with unexecuted source code.

In addition to covering the source code, testers also have to think about missing code. The fact that the "case" statement has no default case could present problems.

Interface

Testing the environment and the source code can be a daunting task. Unfortunately, even after such hard work, there is no guarantee that the code is free of errors. The final consideration is to determine the values assigned to the specific data that crosses the interface from the environment to the software under test.

We begin with variable input (for example, time and date). Variable input is difficult to test because many variable types can assume a wide range of possible values. How many different times are there in a day? The combinations aren't encouraging: There are twelve hours times sixty minutes times sixty seconds times two am/pm settings for a total of 86,400 different input values. That's just the valid ones; invalid times like 29:00 have to be tested too. After we test all these, we have to consider the number of possible values for the date field, both legal and illegal, and decide on specific combinations of time and date to enter simultaneously—like midnight on December 31,1999. This is enough to overwhelm even the biggest testing budget.

The final consideration is to determine the context of the inputs (that is, which inputs will be applied consecutively during testing). This is perhaps the most subtle and elusive aspect of testing.

Obviously, the first input that must be applied is the one that causes the software to be invoked. Next, we must apply one of the other inputs, choose another to follow that one, and so forth until we finally exit the software. Lots of interesting things can happen during such sequencing. Will the software accept several consecutive tab keys? Will it handle a change to the "Time" field only, the "Date" field only, or changes to both? The only way to find out is to apply each of these cases separately.

How many cases are there? Because the "while" loop is unbounded, there is no upper limit. This means that testers must have a way of handling infinite input domains. Two such ways have emerged. First, we might isolate infinite input subsets into separate subdomains, [11] decomposing the problem into smaller problems. Second, just like development, a necessary strategy in testing is abstraction. Testers generally abstract inputs into events. In other words, instead of dealing with specific physical inputs like mouse clicks and keystrokes, testers create abstract events that encompass many physical input sequences. We already did this by creating the inputs "time" and "date." During analysis of the input domain, these abstractions can be used to think through the problem. When the test scenario is actually implemented,[3] testers can replace the abstraction with one of its possible physical instantiations.

---

[3] I use the term "scenario" loosely to mean simply "instructions about what things to test." A more precise term is "test case," which implies exact specification of initial conditions, inputs to apply, and expected outputs.

Testing Terminology

Software testing is often equated with finding bugs. However, test scenarios that do not reveal failures are also informative, so I offer the following definition of software testing: Software testing is the process of executing a software system to determine whether it matches its specification and executes in its intended environment.

The fact the system is *executed* distinguishes testing from code reviews, in which uncompiled source code is read and analyzed statically (usually by developers). Testing, on the other hand, requires a running executable.

A specification is crucial to support testing. It defines correct behavior so that incorrect behavior is easier to identify. Incorrect behavior is referred to as a *failure* of the software. Failures are caused by *faults* in the source code, which are often called *defects* or *bugs*. It is the task of the oracle to compare actual output with specified output to identify failures, and generally, the developer of the code diagnoses the causal fault.

Software can also fail by not satisfying environmental constraints that fall out of the scope of the specification. For example, if the code takes too much memory or executes too slowly, or if the product works on one operating system but not another, these are considered failures.

Software testing is classified according to how testers perform the first two phases of the testing process. The scope of the first phase, modeling the software's environment, determines whether you are doing *unit*, *integration*, or *system* testing.

Unit testing is the testing of individual software components or a collection of components. When unit testing is performed, testers define the input domain for the unit(s) in question and ignore the rest of the system. Unit testing sometimes requires the construction of throwaway driver code and stubs, and it is often performed in a debugger.

Integration testing is the testing of multiple components that have each received prior and separate unit testing. In general, the focus is on the subset of the domain, which represents communication between the components.

System testing is the testing of a collection of components that constitutes a deliverable product. In general, the entire domain must be considered to satisfy the criteria for a system test.

The second phase of testing, test selection, determines what *type* of testing you are doing. There are two main types.

Functional testing requires the selection of test scenarios without regard to the structure of the source code. Thus test-selection methods and test data adequacy criteria must be based on attributes of the specification or operational environment and not on attributes of the code or data structures. Functional testing is also called *specification-based testing*, *behavioral testing*, and *black box testing*.

Structural testing requires that inputs be drawn based solely on the structure of the source code or its data structures. Structural testing is also called *code-based testing* and *white box testing*.

Index

A

acceptance testing, 3
Ada, 5, 16, 32, 151
API, 6–9, 11, 13, 16, 22, 28, 35, 37, 54, 105, 107, 112, 116, 117, 119, 120, 129, 131, 133, 136, 137, 139, 140, 146, 148, 149, 155, 157, 161, 166
Application Program Interface, *see* API
array bounds, 61, 62
ASCII, 102, 129
ASCII character set, 28, 29, 129
assignment statement, 6, 25, 67
automation, 165–167

B

backward compatibility, 100
behavior, 3–5, 9–11, 19, 20, 22, 27–29, 31–34, 36, 41–43, 45, 46, 48, 105, 113, 116, 118, 135, 136, 144, 146, 149, 151, 155, 166, 167, 174
boundary value, 22, 24, 74, 102
boundary value partitioning, 162
buffer overflow, 34, 35
bug fest, 125
bug hunt, 124, 126

C

Canned HEAT, *viii, x, xiii, xiv,* 84, 86, 91, 95, 101, 103, 104, 106–108, 109, 110, 112, 113, 115–118, 120, 139, 140–142, 144–146, 148–151, 153–157 *see also* Hostile Environment Application Tester (HEAT))
capabilities, 5, 6, 11, 12, 14, 15, 19
character set, 28, 29, 33, 97, 102, 129
code review, 3, 174
computation, 12–15, 19, 25, 38, 54, 57, 59, 62, 67, 68, 70–74, 76, 78, 79, 129

conformance testing, 3
control, *xiv,* 22, 27, 28, 46, 107, 108, 110, 113, 130, 133, 154–157
control structure, 38, 129, 130, 164
conventional versus object-oriented programs, 130, 132
corrupt file, 9
cyclical redundancy check, 103, 156

D

damaged disk, 95
data, 5–9, 11–15, 57, 59, 64–68, 73–78, 83, 85, 95, 96, 98, 100–103, 105, 106, 115, 120, 130, 131, 136, 139, 161, 164–166, 168, 173
data constraints, 63, 64
data corruption, 38, 83, 103
data flow, 164, 169
data structure, 12–14, 22, 38, 40, 58, 60, 61–63, 78, 79, 130, 131, 164, 174
data type, 21, 22, 24, 26, 28, 33, 62, 74, 101
database, 6, 7, 11, 125, 132, 136, 161
default value, 25–27, 40, 53
delimiter, *xiv,* 9, 101, 102, 130, 131
design of experiments, 39
device driver, 6, 8, 94, 161
dynamically linked libraries, 7

E

embedded software, 5, 84
environment, *viii, xiv,* 5–8, 10–12, 14, 15, 105–107, 116, 117, 135, 136, 139, 140, 148, 150, 151, 153, 155, 160, 161, 165, 170, 172–174
error case, 21, 22, 37, 43, 62, 85, 106, 135
error-checking code, 12, 68, 85, 161

error code, *xiv*, 8, 10, 11, 20, 21, 85, 95, 99, 101, 119, 130, 136, 137, 139, 151
error-handling code, 74, 85, 94, 95,106, 135, 150, 151
error message, 20–24, 41, 53, 64, 68, 91, 97, 99
exception, *xiv*, 8, 21, 106, 131, 135, 136, 139, 150, 151
exception handler, *xiv*, 21, 68, 74, 99, 131, 150, 151
exception-handling code, 131

F
fault injection, *viii*, *x*, *xiv*, 86, 102, 103, 106, 108, 110, 116–118, 120, 135, 136, 138–140, 148, 151, 152, 154
fault model, *xiii*, 3, 5, 12, 14, 19, 57
fault seeding, 164
feature interaction, 14, 67, 75, 76
file, 5–10, 22, 47, 83, 85, 91, 95–101, 130, 131
file access permission, 99, 100
file-based attack, 83, 95, 103, 104
file extension, 9, 96, 97, 98
file name, 34, 96–99, 153, 162, 163
file permission, 9, 99, 100, 136
file system, 6, 9, 14, 83–85, 91, 107, 136, 156, 163
file system interface, *xiii*, 10, 83, 103, 161
functional code, 21, 135
functional testing, 174

G
general protection violation, 26
genetic algorithms, 162
grammars, 162
graphical user interface, 21, 131, 133, 135, 153
GUI, 8, 9, 12, 16, 22, 37, 40, 51, 52, 100, 105, 129, 131, 133, 161 *see also* graphical user interface
GUI control, 8, 9, 35, 133

H
Holodeck, 117, 118, 148, 149, 150
Hostile Environment Application Tester (HEAT), 11, 106
human interface, 6, 8, 9, 161

I
infinite loop, 71, 72
input, 4–15, 19–22, 25, 26, 28, 29, 31, 33, 37–45, 48, 52–55, 57, 58, 62, 73, 74, 78, 79, 130, 131, 159, 160–164, 168–171, 173, 174
input buffer, 34
input checking, 21
input combination, 4, 9, 12, 37, 39, 42, 44, 45, 97, 159
input domain, 19, 45, 76, 163, 164, 173, 174
input filter, 21
input length, 22
input sequence, 8, 9, 40, 164, 173
input sequencing, 45, 46
input type, 22
input variable, 4, 37, 162
inspection, 3
instruction pointer, 21
integration testing, 174
interface, *viii*, *xiii*, 5–10, 12, 19, 21, 57, 58, 78, 105, 106, 116, 129, 131, 135, 148, 160–162, 164, 170, 172, 173
interoperability, *xiii*, 90, 91, 107, 157
invalid output, 44–46, 64
invocation, 7, 32

K
kernel, 6, 7, 10, 105, 137, 139, 157

L
language theory, 162
long string, 34, 48, 65, 97, 102
loop, 27, 39, 67, 71, 130, 171–173

low memory *xiv,* 10, 108, 109, 115, 137, 140

M
measuring testing progress, 160, 167
media-based attack, 83, 103, 104
memory corruption, 61
memory fault, 91, 107, 112, 140, 144, 157
memory leak, 40, 132
modeling the software's environment, 160, 174
multitasking, 90, 171

N
network fault, 107, 112, 144, 155
null value, 27

O
object-oriented, 5, 129, 130, 166
object-oriented programming paradigm, 132
observe-and-fail attack, 116, 119
operand, 38, 67, 68, 73, 78, 79
operating system, 6, 8, 10, 11, 14, 29, 33, 35, 51, 55, 85, 89–91, 95–97, 99, 160, 161, 167, 170, 171, 174
operating system kernel, 7
operational profile, 128
operator, 16, 67, 68, 73, 78, 79, 151, 163
oracle, *xiv,* 26, 68, 132, 133, 165, 166, 169, 174
other software, 6, 8, 14, 105, 129, 161
output, 6, 12–15, 19, 26, 38, 39, 42–45, 47, 48, 50, 55, 57, 58, 62, 76, 79, 132, 165, 166, 170, 173, 174

P
paging, 46, 132
parameter selection, 9
performance testing, 3

predicate, 6
problem domain, 44, 45, 72
programming languages, 5, 28, 29, 68

R
real-time software, 84
record-and-simulate attack, 106, 119
recursion, 71, 72
refreshing the screen, 51, 52, 54
regression test, *xiv,* 167, 169
regular expression, 32, 162
reliability, *xiv,* 16, 119, 120, 151, 168, 169
reliability model, 168, 169
reliability testing, 3
requirements, 3, 4, 19, 20, 119, 135
robustness, 119, 120, 135, 151
robustness testing, 3
running and evaluating test scenarios, 160, 165
runtime libraries, 6, 11

S
safety-critical application, 95, 151
screen refresh, 40, 52, 132
security, 32, 36, 70, 117, 130, 149
seeded error, 164, 168
selecting test scenarios, 160, 163
simulated environment, 3
software interface, 105, 159, 161
software testing process, 160
source code, 3, 10, 136, 139, 151, 163, 164, 168, 170–172, 174
special character, 28, 102, 129
specification, 3, 19, 44, 165, 166, 169, 173, 174
state, 4, 21, 43, 112, 165–167
stochastic processes, 162
stored data, 4, 12–14, 40, 47, 57, 59, 64, 67, 74, 135
string, 8, 9, 11, 28–36, 49, 53, 55, 101, 102
system, 86, 101

system call, 10, 29, 117–119, 132, 133,
        137, 149, 150
system-call interception, 137
system input, 10, 133
system testing, 174

T
Task Manager, 33, 90, 154
test data adequacy criteria, 163–165,
        167, 168, 174
test verification, 133
testability, 151, 168

U
unexpected return values, 101
unhandled exception, 101

UNICODE, 102, 129
UNICODE character set, 28
unit testing, 61, 71, 85, 174
user interface, *viii, xiii,* 19, 48, 53, 57,
        67, 78, 83, 102, 163
user interface controls, 130, 133
user manual, 3

V
variable, 25–27, 32, 38, 53, 162, 163,
        165, 173

W
white box testing, 12, 106, 174
Windows® kernel, 7, 10

Notes

Notes

010101011011000100100100101010110110001001001001010101
Notes

Notes

Notes

Notes

01010101101100010010010010101011011000100100100101010 1

Notes

Notes

License Agreement

The software on the attached CD is a research prototype developed by faculty and students at Florida Tech and may contain copyrighted or patented code. It is offered "as is" for the purpose of reproducing the attacks published in this book and for experimentation by the reader on their own software products. The author and publisher make no warranties and accept no liabilities arising from use or misuse of the products.

By installing the applications on the CD, the reader accepts these terms.

CD Contents

Canned HEAT v.2.0 is a runtime fault injection tool that allows testers to simulate faulty software environments (e.g., low memory, congested network and low disk space).

Installer Details

The file "CH3 Setup.exe" in the "Canned HEAT" directory must be executed in order to install the application. The installer for Canned HEAT is very basic and simply asks the target for the application files.

For further information visit:

Canned HEAT Web Site: **http://se.fit.edu/cannedheat**

Holodeck Lite v 1.0 incorporates all of the fault injection capability of Canned HEAT and adds logging capabilities for debugging and fault isolation.

Installer Details

The Holodeck installer is very much like a Windows Installer you would normally see from most commercial applications. It is very simple to follow and simply requires the execution of the "holodeck_lite-02132002.exe" file in the "Holodeck Lite" directory.

For further information visit:

Holodeck Web Site: **http://se.fit.edu/holodeck**

System Requirements for Canned HEAT and Holodex Lite

Operating System: Windows 2000 (Professional, Server, Advanced Server), Windows XP (Home, Professional), Windows .NET Server (2002)

Pentium 200mHz w/ 64MB RAM (minimum); Pentium II 400 w/ 128MB RAM (recommended)

This software does NOT WORK on Windows NT or Windows 95/98/Me.

This book comes with a CD that contains two very useful testing tools that were written by faculty and students at Florida Tech.

In addition, *www.HowToBreakSoftware.com* is your online gateway to the latest tool updates, bug stories, and technology announcements related to the discipline of breaking software.